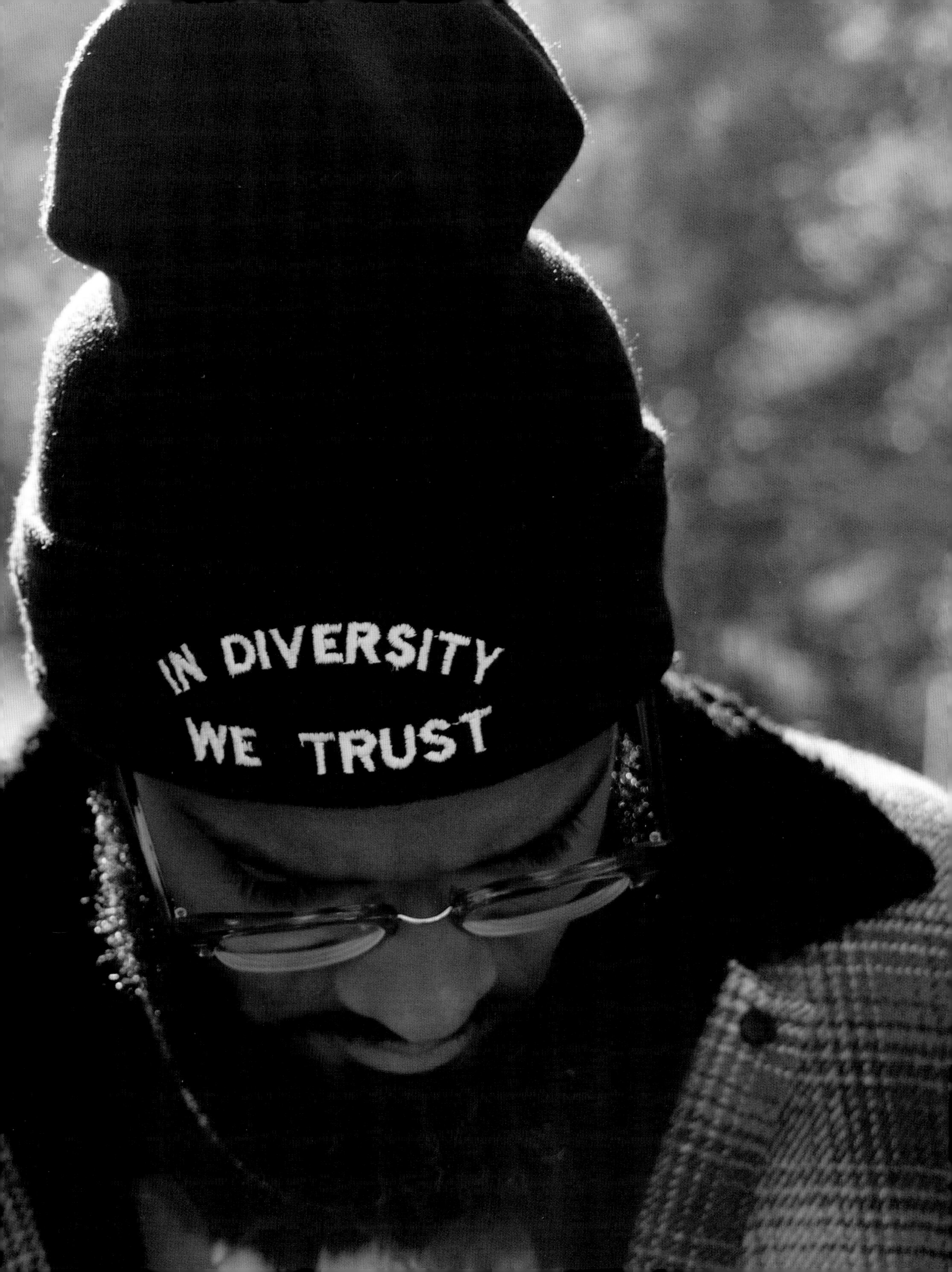
IN DIVERSITY
WE TRUST

NORTHERN SOUL

SOUTHERN-INSPIRED HOME COOKING FROM A NORTHERN KITCHEN

Justin Sutherland

FOREWORD BY KWAME ONWUACHI

HARVARD
COMMON
PRESS

Inspiring | Educating | Creating | Entertaining

Brimming with creative inspiration, how-to projects, and useful information to enrich your everyday life, quarto.com is a favorite destination for those pursuing their interests and passions.

First Published in 2022 by The Harvard Common Press, an imprint of The Quarto Group, 100 Cummings Center, Suite 265-D, Beverly, MA 01915, USA.
T (978) 282-9590 F (978) 283-2742 Quarto.com

The Harvard Common Press titles are also available at discount for retail, wholesale, promotional, and bulk purchase. For details, contact the Special Sales Manager by email at specialsales@quarto.com or by mail at The Quarto Group, Attn: Special Sales Manager, 100 Cummings Center, Suite 265-D, Beverly, MA 01915, USA.

26 25 24 23 22   1 2 3 4 5

ISBN: 978-0-7603-7532-7

Digital edition published in 2022
eISBN: 978-0-7603-7533-4

Library of Congress Cataloging-in-Publication Data available

Design: Tanya Jacobson, jcbsn.co
Cover Image: Asha Belk
Page Layout: Cindy Samargia Laun
Photography: Asha Belk; except Shutterstock on page 32, 198, 100; and courtesy of author on page 1, 12, 15, 19, 38, 75, 107, 134, 140

Printed in China

DEDICATION

For Zona Sutherland and Burnell Blagsvedt

CONTENTS

FOREWORD BY KWAME ONWUACHI

I think a chef is born not trained. A future leader can be easily identified even as a child: This is someone who goes against the grain, and someone others listen to. The cooking part is easy. Being the person who can inspire others, however, even when they struggle to see the full vision, that takes something special. For Chef Justin Sutherland, being this kind of leader has come naturally. Chef Justin is not only at the helm of several restaurants but has been able to grace your television screens with ease for years now. In so doing he has solidified himself as someone to pay attention to, someone to remember for decades to come. Maybe it was the cold winters in Minnesota that ushered in warm bowls of pork chili to ease the winter frost. Or maybe it was the summers spent in the South, running through the sorghum fields and picking green beans on the stoop. Or perhaps it was a small cup of dashi sipped slowly with his Japanese grandmother. These are the experiences that gave him the confidence to pick up an apron and tell his own story. However it happened, I am glad it did.

The word *soul* can evoke many different emotions, and different meanings, depending on who you ask. To some it refers to that inner spirit that represents who we actually are, a deeper level of our subconscious that transcends flesh and common conjecture. Now the soul of one's cooking does just that. You are not just cooking for perfect seasoning (which should be a prerequisite) but to share a story or an anecdote with someone. You combine those two things—cooking for flavor and cooking to share your soul—and you have this cookbook. This is a book that perfectly weaves Justin's Minnesota influences with his Southern roots, which are deeply wrapped around food knowledge and culture. When I first pick up a cookbook, the thing that crosses my mind is, well, will I actually cook from this? Will this be a book that remains buried in my library, or something that stays near the kitchen? Will this be something that I refer to other chefs as a benchmark to the type of cuisine it represents? In the case of this book, the answer is a resounding yes.

You can tell in this book that Chef Justin cooks and writes about foods that he just loves to eat. It comes across in lots of places, from his introductions to his appetizer recipes, for example, or in the wonderful way he describes eating in Spain. Dishes in this book like Chef Justin's supple BBQ oysters and his whipped pimiento cheese, and so many others, are layered in flavor but also in history. They are not only deliciously put together, with every ingredient adding another note to the symphony of flavors, but thoughtful in their origins. When you pay attention to how a chef is composing their dish under a close eye, you can see the main ingredient in plain sight: care.

Southern traditions matched with contemporary cooking techniques make any of these dishes easy for the home cook to execute. Whether you're cooking for yourself or want to totally impress your guests, just flip through the pages of this book and there is something for you. To write a cookbook that has something for everyone, and for any occasion, is a balancing act more difficult than Cirque du Soleil, but Chef Justin has pulled it off. Keep this book close by and you'll be able to impress the pickiest eaters. This is a multilayered lexicon of American classics done his way.

Rarely does someone's first cookbook stand out from the crowd as this one does. It is a testament to Justin Sutherland's extraordinary culinary prowess. I encourage you to start with the rubs and pickles recipes, and then to work your way through the rest of the book. Each dish is a love letter to Justin's past; and each one is like a paper airplane gracefully floating into the kitchens of future cooks. If you have haven't tasted his food before, get ready for something special. In the famous words of The Notorious B.I.G., "If you don't know, now you know."

INTRODUCTION
THE SOUL OF THE SOUTH
IN THE HEART OF THE NORTH

A dear friend of mine often says, "Everything good in my life started over a meal." No words ever rang truer.

Forget math—food is the universal language. Food is so much more than a means to an end. More than just the calories and nutrients that sustain our physical lives, food is a fuel that powers us spiritually and emotionally, too. Food tells a story, evokes memories, bridges gaps, and connects humanity by a singular thread.

My love affair with food and my journey down this career path started very young. As a child, I loved to eat. Food was everything to me. In fact, it's been said that my first word was *bread.* It's hard to find a picture of me as a toddler without a piece of bread in my hand or my mouth. My favorite toys were the pots and pans and wooden spoons in the kitchen. At age five, when most boys wanted a new Tonka truck, I asked for an Easy-Bake Oven. I received one and I used it to create my first masterpiece, a chocolate cake baked with the heat of a 100-watt lightbulb.

From the beginning, the near-sacred importance of sitting down to a meal as a family was ingrained in me. My parents divorced when I was young. My mother, who was a flight attendant and often traveling, still always made sure we sat down at the dinner table and ate together. Even preparing for and cleaning up after the meal was a family affair: One brother set the table, one cleared the table, and one swept the floor, and everyone helped with the dishes (although not without the occasional pushback). Our meals were never fancy, and my mother's signature dishes are still my three favorite meals of all time—but *only* when cooked by her: spaghetti with meat sauce, tater-tot hot-dish with chicken and broccoli, and her famous fried rice.

In addition to daily dinners with my immediate family, holidays, celebrations, and get-togethers with our extended family also were important, both for the human connections and for the food. From Easter to Christmas, Sunday brunches to celebrations of school accomplishments, my grandparents, aunts, uncles, and cousins always made a point to break bread together. The meals were generally home cooked, because we did not grow up with much money. A dinner out was considered a special treat. And when we did go out to eat, our fine dining was at Red Lobster, Olive Garden, TGI Fridays, and, maybe a few times a year, the teppanyaki table at Ichiban. The type of cuisine did not matter; what mattered was being together.

Even when I would eat by myself, sitting down in what I took to be the proper manner mattered to me. My grandmother often took care of me while my mother was flying around the world serving others in the sky to support us. For a long period during my childhood, a show called *Eureeka's Castle* aired on Nickelodeon at 11 o'clock each morning. At the start of the show, the character would ring a bell and yell, "Lunchtime!" I was always ready, with my little blue Fisher-Price table positioned perfectly in front of the television, meticulously set with silverware and a glass of milk. At the moment "Lunchtime!" was yelled, my grandmother, as if a character in the show herself, would set down in front of me the lunch I ate every day: two hot dogs (with no bun), each topped with a slice of American cheese, generously sprinkled with dried minced onions and Lawry's seasoned salt, and garnished with scallions. All plated on a now-collectible McDonald's plate—which I should have held on to, because the last time I checked, someone paid $500 for one on eBay.

This hot dog plate is a snack I still make for myself to this day. Every time I take the first bite, my eyes well up as I remember how much that meal meant to me as a child and how much love that simple dish carried with it. It wasn't about the ingredients, it was loosely about the place, but it was mostly about the hands that prepared it.

It was always apparent how much "mealtime" was a part of our family. It wasn't until I started eating at friends' houses at sleepovers that I realized how special our mealtime really was. I come from a very diverse and multicultural family. On my mother's side, my grandmother Masako came to this country from Japan during the Korean War speaking no English and at a time when the United States had poor relations, to say the least, with Japan. She wasn't allowed to bring any of her culture to this country for fear of repercussions from the United States government. My grandfather on that side is a 6-foot, 5-inch Viking of Norwegian descent, a product of the Great Depression, from a family of farmers and carpenters.

On my father's side, I am the descendant of slaves and sharecroppers. My grandfather, Harold, came up from Mississippi and settled in Waterloo, Iowa, with my Grandma Zona. Food was Zona's love language and her food was the start of my love of soul food and barbecue.

It was the combined cultures of my family that gave me my first glimpse into the vast possibilities that foods brought to the world. The day I realized that not all family dinners consisted of Southern collard greens, Japanese sushi, and Norwegian *lefse* (a potato flatbread), all together on the same table, was the first time I realized we were different. I loved it and I wanted to learn and experience more.

With my Grandma Masako unable to truly share her culture, or even to teach her own children her language, her food was the gateway to her story. At a young age, I followed her around the kitchen, tasting everything from rice balls filled with pickled plums to *somen*—or, as we called them, "summer noodles"—pickled daikon and mochi, to tonkatsu and, my all-time favorite, sukiyaki, a one-pot family-style dish that filled my brothers and me with so much joy every time she shared it. Whenever we could, we would invite our white American friends to her house to share our grandmother with them and let them experience this magic in a pot.

Burnell, my Norwegian grandfather, taught me the importance of respecting food. He taught me that no meal was ever complete without a slice of bread with butter and a glass of cold milk. As a product of a farming family during the Depression, he instilled in all of us the rule that we must never waste food, and, if food was prepared for you, you ate it all. Even when he became financially secure, he still would cut the mold off a block of cheese, because the rest of it was still good and not to be wasted. And you never left the table until your plate was clean.

Burnell gave me an appreciation for good, wholesome Midwest comfort food. He was all meat and potatoes. His wife, my Japanese grandmother, learned how to prepare pot roast, Swedish meatballs, spare ribs with sauerkraut, and meatloaf. Burnell and I would make a weekly trip to the VFW post for the lutefisk dinner—the lye-soaked fish covered in a mystery white sauce alongside what had to be boxed white potatoes. But I always cleaned my plate, because that's what you did when you ate with Grandpa. These foods were humble, but to this day, they always remind me of the importance of respecting food. Nothing must be wasted, and a meal is never complete without bread and butter.

Grandma Zona was the Big Mama to her neighborhood. She was a mother to so many neighborhood kids and, although she never had a lot of money, she always made sure that anyone and everyone who came to her table was fed. From church basement lunches (which were sorely needed after a five-hour Methodist service) to Saturday cookouts to every meal in between, she loved to cook, she loved to serve food, and she loved to protect.

It was something of a culture shock when we would travel from our suburban life in Apple Valley, Minnesota, to visit Grandma Zona in what, in my young mind, was "the hood." There was clearly a disparity between what I had at home and what I experienced in her neighborhood. But I found a very tight-knit and connected community there. It gave me a chance to experience a different way of life—sitting on the front stoop shooting dice, foolishly playing chicken with oncoming trains, or riding bikes to the corner store to get my uncle a pack of cigarettes, knowing I would be able to keep the change to buy a couple Laffy Taffy candies or Lemonheads. With my brothers and cousins, I explored the many abandoned houses and we would take off running when we found a squatter. It was such a different life from where I lived, but I loved it.

All of the happiness and connection in this community was most visible in its food, and especially its soul food. In Grandma Zona's kitchen, it seemed as if there was always a pot of collard greens on the stove, someone cleaning chitlins with a toothbrush, and a vat of hot oil just waiting for perfectly breaded chicken to be submerged.

Then there were the barbecues. Now, we aren't talking about the weekend warriors with their Big Green Eggs or other trendy smokers or grills in the driveway. This was the whole neighborhood coming together at a local park to cook, commune, and throw the fuck down. It was the deacons from church alongside the neighborhood drug dealers, gang members of different affiliations, absent fathers, and baby mamas—and everyone was somehow your cousin. They all put everything aside to come together to grill and eat. My uncle Hawkeye always manned the grill with his

40-ounce beer in one hand and the barbecue didn't stop until there were no more coals.

On barbecue days, I made countless bike rides to the corner store after hearing, "Boy, dem coals are still hot, you better go get some more meat." Ribs, chicken, pork chops, wings, hot dogs, it didn't matter—if the coals were glowing, we were still cooking. Then came the sides. Mac 'n' cheese, which I quickly learned not just anyone can bring to the barbecue—and, if you fuck it up once, don't bother trying it again. Collard greens, chitlins, black-eyed peas, potato salad, yams, the list goes on. This food spoke to me. It was something more than a meal. It had heart. It tasted like family. But what it really was all about, I believe, was that it had soul.

My life continued on this path, in which the love of food shared with my family was at the center of everything that mattered, for many years. Eventually my Grandma Zona passed away, followed by my Grandpa Burnell. But the lessons they taught and the food memories never leave—they only grow stronger over time.

As I matured, I became not just an observer of food but an active student of it. I ate everything I could, everywhere I could. I especially found myself wanting to learn more about the South, about soul food—the food that spoke to me most.

When I decided to turn food into a career, I moved to Atlanta. I had gone earlier to business school, but at the suggestion of my father, Kerry, and with a lot of encouragement from him and others, I decided to pivot in a new direction and go to culinary school. I chose Atlanta because I wanted to be close to the foods of the South and the people who mastered them. I began to explore firsthand the dining and cooking of the South, from New Orleans to St. Louis, Mississippi to Georgia, Alabama to Texas. Spending time in these places filled my nose with the smells of soulful foods. It filled my stomach with their flavors. And it fed my soul.

When I moved back home to Minnesota and decided to open my first restaurant, Handsome Hog, the most important thing for me was to share those feelings and experiences. As my Grandma Zona had done for me, I wanted to welcome everyone to my table and help feed their souls.

I want to pay homage to the memories and the feelings of that soul food. I want to tell the history of this food, its stories, its origins, and the pride and pain it represents.

This is food that was smuggled into the United States by my ancestors—beans and seeds hidden in the hair of West African women in the slave trade who were stolen from their homes as labor to build this country. And this food encompasses the unwanted scraps that were discarded and left to our people—and that have now become sought-after delicacies. This is food that was enjoyed in generations of Southern restaurants, with white owners in the front while the true culinary geniuses worked out of sight in the back. In this book, I tell these stories through the lens of *all* of my experiences, not just my origin and my family, but also through my training in classic French cuisine and fine dining, and my many years of national and international travel (for which I thank my flight attendant mother).

As a born Northerner, this is the food that resonates with me, that feeds my soul. The recipes within this book are the stories of my life.

Justin

Spices,

Sauces,

Rubs

The deep, layered flavors found in many of the protein preparations offered in this book are provided by rubs and spice mixes—ground spices, chiles, and dried herbs mixed in varying proportions and sometimes augmented with salts, sugars, or citrus.

As with practicing any craft, you need to select, or in some cases create, the right tool for the right job. When it comes to protein preparation, rubs, spice mixes, and sauces for a cook are like the bass line or the beat to a DJ—lay the right ones down in the right places for the right amount of time, and you'll get everybody in the groove.

Rubs in particular make you participate in the very tactile practice of cooking. Whether you put on a pair of gloves or not (and in the recipes using chile-heavy rubs I recommend you do!), in order to get an even layer on the exterior of the cut you've chosen, you need to engage in the visceral experience of laying your hands on the food you are preparing. The act of massaging those flavors into the meat is one more way of adding your dedication and care—your soul—into the meal you're preparing. Make time for that prep. Don't get yourself in a hurry. I don't care what anyone says: when the cook really cares, the food tastes better, smells better, and makes you feel better.

The two rubs in this book are a pair of my favorite recipes. My staff and I have spent years experimenting with them and improving them, to the point where I've actually developed a branded line I use in my kitchens and offer up for sale to the public. But, like all of the recipes in the following pages, they now belong to you and your kitchen. The heat can be toned up or down by reducing or increasing the amount of cayenne or ground chiles. Feel free to experiment by reducing or increasing any of the ingredients, or by adding your own. You're driving the boat now, Hoss.

Bourbon BBQ Sauce

3 cups (710 ml) bourbon

2 cups (480 g) ketchup

1⅔ cups (375 g) packed
light brown sugar

½ cup (170 g) unsulphured molasses

½ cup (120 ml) Worcestershire sauce

1¼ cups (295 ml) malt vinegar

4 teaspoons (20 ml) liquid smoke

4 teaspoons (10 g) onion powder

2½ teaspoons (5 g) freshly
ground black pepper

**MAKES ABOUT
4⅔ CUPS (1 KG)**

When I first opened Handsome Hog, I was determined to introduce traditional Southern barbecue flavors and technique to Saint Paul, which meant the meat and the pickles would work together to properly showcase and complement the flavors. I didn't want my barbecue to be about the sauce, but my fellow Minnesotans, for better or worse, rose up with a hue and cry demand for a brown sugar and molasses, KC-style barbecue sauce. The end result was the following recipe—tangy, sweet, and smoky with a latent black pepper punch and flavored with a hefty portion of bourbon whiskey. Stir this one carefully, low and slow, until reduced by about half. Otherwise it boils over and makes a mess, if not a fire. Bourbon belongs in your warm and grateful belly, not on your stovetop. This sauce really shines on barbecued beef brisket, but it goes well with chicken and pork as well.

INSTRUCTIONS ───────────

1. Combine the bourbon, ketchup, brown sugar, molasses, Worcestershire sauce, vinegar, liquid smoke, onion powder, and black pepper in a large pot. Whisk together. Simmer over medium to medium-low heat until reduced by half, about 90 minutes. Caution: If the sauce reaches a boil, immediately turn off the heat and remove it from the burner because it will boil over if unattended. When finished, the sauce should be a glossy, dark mahogany and cling to the back of a spoon.

2. Allow the sauce to cool, then transfer to an airtight container to store in your refrigerator. Bring to room temperature before serving at the table alongside any barbecued meat.

Cajun Seasoning

½ cup plus 2 tablespoons (53 g)
ground cayenne

¼ cup (75 g) kosher salt

¼ cup (36 g) garlic powder

¼ cup (28 g) sweet paprika

2 tablespoons (14 g) onion powder

2 tablespoons (5 g) dried thyme

2 tablespoons (6 g) dried oregano

2 tablespoons (12 g) freshly
ground black pepper

**MAKES ABOUT
2 CUPS (229 G)**

For a lot of midwestern and North Country diners, some of their first introductions to an "exotic cuisine" came in the form of Cajun cooking, either at an adventurous restaurant or from a spice shaker from a supermarket shelf. All of the ingredients in this recipe should be stocked in your pantry for use individually from time to time, so picking up any you may be missing is doing yourself as great a favor as keeping this blend at the ready for all sorts of meat, vegetables, and seafood that make their way into your kitchen.

INSTRUCTIONS ───────────

1. Mix together the cayenne, salt, garlic powder, paprika, onion powder, thyme, oregano, and pepper in a bowl.

2. Use immediately or transfer to an airtight container and store in a cool, dark place for up to 4 weeks.

Brisket Rub

1¼ cups (180 g) mustard powder

⅔ cup (201 g) kosher salt

6½ tablespoons (46 g) sweet paprika

⅓ cup (38 g) ground cinnamon

⅓ cup (32 g) freshly
ground black pepper

⅓ cup (48 g) garlic powder

½ cup plus 2 tablespoons (140 g)
packed light brown sugar

**MAKES ABOUT 4½ CUPS
(680 G), ENOUGH FOR ABOUT
2 MEDIUM BRISKETS**

I like a healthy amount of brown sugar in my brisket rub. It adds to the texture of the bark—that dark, smoky crust that develops during the higher heat of the roasting and braising process.

INSTRUCTIONS ───────────

1. Mix together the mustard powder, salt, paprika, cinnamon, black pepper, garlic powder, and brown sugar in a bowl until fully combined.

2. Use immediately or store in an airtight container in a cool, dark place for up to 4 weeks.

Chicken Dredge

6 cups (750 g) all-purpose flour

¾ cup plus 2½ tablespoons
(104 g) cake flour

6 tablespoons plus ½ teaspoon
(43 g) smoked paprika

5 tablespoons (30 g) freshly
ground black pepper

3 tablespoons plus 1 teaspoon
(63 g) kosher salt

3 tablespoons plus 1 teaspoon
(30 g) garlic powder

3 tablespoons plus 1 teaspoon
(23 g) onion powder

1½ teaspoons cayenne pepper

**MAKES ABOUT
8 CUPS (1.04 KG)**

Don't ever be afraid to make this recipe in bulk. It's delicious and all-purpose, particularly when you master the double-dredge technique. In addition to being useful for fried chicken, it can also be used for fried shrimp or oysters.

INSTRUCTIONS ——————————

1. Sift the all-purpose flour, cake flour, paprika, black pepper, salt, garlic powder, onion powder, and cayenne into a large mixing bowl and stir until fully combined.

2. Use immediately or transfer to an airtight container and store in a cool, dark place for up to 4 weeks.

North Carolina Vinegar BBQ Sauce

1 cup (235 ml) white wine vinegar

1 cup (240 ml) apple cider vinegar

¼ cup (60 g) ketchup

¼ cup (44 g) yellow mustard

3 tablespoons (45 g) packed
dark brown sugar

1 tablespoon (19 g) kosher salt

1 tablespoon (7 g) sweet paprika

1½ teaspoons red pepper flakes

1 teaspoon liquid smoke

**MAKES 3 CUPS (750 G),
ENOUGH FOR ABOUT 2 MEDIUM
PORK SHOULDERS**

No cookbook that includes barbecue recipes is complete without giving props to the red chile and vinegar table sauce associated with North Carolina whole-hog barbecues. The dynamic, sharp, bright heat of this concoction was first used to cut through the smoke and fattiness of the meat so the flavor could be properly savored. Use this rendition sparingly at first, maybe even as a dipping sauce on the side. You'll finding yourself building a craving for it, and you'll want to slather it on just about any animal protein making its way to your mouth. Trust me on this one. History is on my side.

INSTRUCTIONS ——————————

1. Combine the white wine vinegar, apple cider vinegar, ketchup, mustard, brown sugar, salt, paprika, red pepper, and liquid smoke in a bowl.

2. Whisk together until well blended.

3. Transfer to an airtight container and store in your refrigerator for up to 3 weeks.

Rib Rub

¾ cup (170 g) packed
dark brown sugar

½ cup (56 g) smoked paprika

½ cup (150 g) kosher salt

¼ cup (21 g) cayenne pepper

¼ cup (36 g) garlic powder

¼ cup (28 g) onion powder

2 tablespoons (11 g) ground ginger

2 tablespoons (12 g) freshly
ground black pepper

2 tablespoons (18 g) mustard powder

**MAKES ABOUT
2¾ CUPS (502 G)**

**THE
RECIPE FOR
BBQ RIBS
IS ON
PAGE 139.**

I've worked on this recipe for almost as long as I kept a roof over my head with a towel and sauté pan in one hand and a pair of tongs in the other. Ribs are one of the great loves of my life, and like in any romantic relationship, it's important to treat your partner in passion with all the love and attention you've got. Even after we opened the doors at Handsome Hog, this recipe continued to evolve until we nailed down the right balance of hot pepper heat and sweetness that would caramelize into a robust bark on the ribs during the smoking and grilling process. At one point, we were literally preparing gallons of this rub at a time, so I contacted a good friend in St. Michael, Minnesota, and they started packaging the recipe for us. If you love barbecue ribs as deeply as I do, you'll understand why all of that attention and evolution is so important. You'll also understand that ribs can be deeply personal, which is why I'm sharing this recipe with you. I care about your ribs, too—and if you don't like as much cayenne, paprika, or garlic as I do, simply tone down your next batch to adjust. However, if we do end up on the same page, feel free to slide into https://justinsutherland.com/shop/ and save yourself a little effort.

INSTRUCTIONS ———————

1. Combine the brown sugar, paprika, salt, cayenne, garlic powder, onion powder, ginger, black pepper, and mustard powder in a mixing bowl.

2. Stir together until well blended.

3. Use immediately or transfer to an airtight container and store in a cool, dark place for up to 4 weeks.

Chicken Salt

½ **pound (225 g)** chicken skin

½ **cup (125 g)** powdered dried mushrooms (see Note below)

½ **cup plus 2 tablespoons (188 g)** kosher salt

2 tablespoons plus 2½ teaspoons (20 g) white pepper, preferably freshly ground

2 tablespoons (18 g) garlic powder

2 tablespoons (14 g) onion powder

MAKES ABOUT 3 CUPS (590 G)

This recipe is an umami-bomb we developed in the kitchen of Handsome Hog a few years back. The technique and extra steps involved yield a great staple that adds loads of flavor to everything from vegetables to seafood. If you don't want to start hoarding boneless, skinless breasts in your freezer or host a fat-free poultry BBQ, your local butcher will almost always be ready to sell you a stash of chicken skin for this recipe.

INSTRUCTIONS

1. Line a baking sheet with parchment paper and preheat the oven to 175°F (79°C).

2. Scrape all the excess fat from the chicken skins with a bench scraper or butter knife. Arrange the skin in a single layer on the prepared baking sheet and bake until completely dehydrated and crisp, about 5 hours. Allow to cool to room temperature.

3. Combine the dried chicken skin with the powdered mushrooms, salt, white pepper, garlic powder, and onion powder in a food processor and pulse until super finely ground. Use immediately or store in an airtight container in your refrigerator.

   Note: For powdered mushrooms, the best choice is porcini powder, which can be expensive or hard to find, so feel free to substitute a different dried mushroom instead—shiitake being our first recommendation. And if you can't find mushroom powder, buy dried mushrooms and powder them in a blender or spice grinder.

THE LIFE SPAN OF SPICES

There's a misconception among a lot of home cooks that spices last for years. They don't. After a couple of months, most open containers of dry spices will begin a quick slide toward tastelessness. Store them in a cool, dark place, tightly sealed, preferably in a glass jar. Plastic is fine, but it can both absorb and impart flavor into your rubs. Glass—or stainless steel—won't do that.

There's an old French kitchen adage that declares "an ounce of sauce kills a pound of sin"—basically saying that scorched, subpar, or neglected ingredients can be fixed by drowning them in sauce. Case in point would be the numerous cans of creamy mushroom soup that get dumped into the old-school, Minnesotan's go-to family gathering centerpiece, Tater Tot Hot Dish.

As you keep reading, you'll learn that the purist in me, after discovering real heritage Carolina barbecue, didn't even want to offer a barbecue sauce on the menu at my first restaurant, Handsome Hog, for that very reason. I wanted you to taste the love and care my staff, my ancestors, and I were putting into the preparation of the delicious creatures we were roasting, grilling, and smoking. Those old-time, Low Country vinegar-based sauces are there to augment, not overpower.

I'm going to challenge you to put more time, attention, and TLC into your meat and vegetables and rethink what sauces mean to your food. You can put lipstick on a pig or you can dunk a dry chicken wing in a honey barbecue sauce, the results are going to be the same.

The spices, rubs, and sauces in this chapter are here to make your efforts shine. Think of them as the new, sized-down outfit you buy yourself as a reward for all your effort paying off at the gym.

Tennessee Hot

2 cups **(410 g)** lard or
vegetable shortening

1½ cups **(127 g)** cayenne pepper

¾ cup **(170 g)** packed
dark brown sugar

½ cup **(72 g)** garlic powder

¼ cup **(29 g)** smoked paprika

1 tablespoon plus 2 teaspoons **(13 g)**
chili powder

2½ teaspoons **(16 g)** kosher salt

2½ teaspoons **(5 g)** freshly
ground black pepper

**MAKES ABOUT
4⅔ CUPS (842 G)**

If you're not the type to render your own lard or bacon fat,
it's easily found at your local butcher shop. You can also
venture to your nearest Latin American grocery, where it is
sold in butter-sized bricks as *Manteca* for making tamales.

INSTRUCTIONS ——————

1. Warm the lard until just melted in a small saucepan over low heat.

2. Whisk in the cayenne, brown sugar, garlic powder, paprika, chili
    powder, kosher salt, and black pepper until smooth.

3. Use immediately or transfer to an airtight container and store
    in your refrigerator for up to 3 weeks.

4. Before using, put it back into a saucepan and warm over low
    heat until fully melted.

South Carolina Mustard BBQ Sauce

2 cups (352 g) yellow mustard

1 cup (240 ml) apple cider vinegar

½ cup (170 g) honey

¼ cup (60 g) packed light brown sugar

¼ cup (60 ml) Worcestershire sauce

2 tablespoons (30 g) ketchup

1 tablespoon plus 1 teaspoon (20 g) habanero hot sauce, such as Cry Baby Craig's Hot Sauce

2 teaspoons garlic powder

**MAKES ABOUT
4¼ CUPS (1.06 KG)**

We hear a lot in American history about the Pennsylvania Dutch, but there was a substantial settlement of German-speaking immigrants who made their homes—and their tables—in the Carolinas during the eighteenth and nineteenth centuries, particularly in South Carolina. They brought with them a taste for all kinds of vinegars and mustard sauces from their home country that married in a variety of ways with the food they found in their new home. Hot chile peppers eventually made their way into those concoctions that were used to augment and cut through the smoky, unctuous flavors of the barbecued meats, pork in particular, featured at the feasts for which their homes became famous. Carolina barbecue sauce is widely recognized as the granddaddy, the original, the O.G. Seems in this case the "G" stands for "German."

INSTRUCTIONS ———————————

1. Combine the mustard, vinegar, honey, brown sugar, Worcestershire sauce, ketchup, hot sauce, and garlic powder in a bowl.

2. Whisk until smooth.

3. Use immediately or transfer to an airtight container and store in your refrigerator for up to 3 weeks.

PICKLED

THINGS

2

When I was growing up in Minnesota, most of the pickling I saw was limited to cucumbers and beets. Occasionally someone's mom or grandmother would have pickled green beans in the pantry. It wasn't until I moved to Atlanta after high school that I discovered the pantheon of pickled fruits and vegetables that are requisite elements in any meal celebrating Southern foodways. Tasting pickled peaches for the first time blew my mind—and the more I became interested in food and where it came from, the more I wanted to learn about how food was pickled and why. My curiosity likely also stems from the fact that three of the major cuisines on the planet that rely upon and celebrate pickles and pickling as part of a balanced meal (Southern African American, Asian, and Scandinavian) are cooked by the people from whom I receive the lion's share of my DNA.

In all of these cultures, climate and the length of the growing season created the necessity to preserve food. In Asia and in the Southern United States, sweltering heat and an absence of refrigeration accelerated spoilage of ingredients in peak season. Pickles, preserves, and fermentation were the most reliable ways to slow or eliminate that process. In my neck of the woods and in northern Europe, vegetables were pickled at the peak of a very short growing season so they could still contribute nutrition, such as much-needed vitamin C, to meals throughout our frigid winters.

Pickled, fermented, and preserved foods will always be celebrated in the foods I bring to the table simply because they are luscious and flavorful. They add balance to a meal without overseasoning any individual dish or preparation. While salt, acidity, and sweetness are necessary elements in any pickling recipe, the proportions in which they are used should differ from item to item, vegetable to vegetable, fruit to fruit (and even proteins can be pickled). The Minnesota dive bar fan in me couldn't let this portion of the book pass without at least mentioning pickled

eggs and pickled pigs' feet. What's more, the way those elements of salt, acidity, and sweetness are used in the recipe won't just depend on the fruit or vegetable itself, it will also depend on the time of the season—and even what kind of season you're having. Green tomatoes, peaches, and strawberries are perfect examples: if you're having a long, hot spring and summer, the sweetness of these fruits (yes, tomatoes are fruit—even green ones. Don't argue with me) will be more pronounced, and you will want to use less sugar in the pickling brine in order for their flavors to truly shine. If the season is a little cool, you'll likely do the reverse.

In short, this section of the book says a lot about how I hope you'll learn to cook after reading it—with an understanding of and respect for individual ingredients and the confidence to tailor recipes to your own sense of flavor. Go to the grocery store just before you know a certain ingredient will be in season. Get some pears in July, strawberries in April, or a watermelon in May if you can find one. The pickling process is as versatile as you should be. Play around and experiment with your preferences.

Pickled Cucumbers

Three variations on a necessity in any home or restaurant kitchen. The Bread and Butter Pickles (page 42) presented here would get a thumbs-up from any Scandinavian granny worth her North Country apron strings and you could open your own deli with the Dill Pickles recipe (opposite)—you'll just have to follow up by sourcing a world-class pumpernickel. My favorites by far are the Spicy Cucumber Pickles (below). They're a lot like me after a long day on the St. Croix River when I have access to bottomless tumblers of bourbon cocktails.

1¼ cups (294 ml) water

½ cup plus 2 tablespoons (148 ml) white vinegar

1 cup (200 g) sugar

5 chiles de árbol, coarsely chopped

⅓ cup (78 ml) hot sauce, preferably Cry Baby Craig's Hot Sauce, or your favorite bottled habanero hot sauce

½ medium yellow onion, coarsely chopped

2 garlic cloves, smashed

2 fronds fresh dill

2½ tablespoons (47 g) kosher salt

½ teaspoon smoked paprika

½ teaspoon dill seeds

3 seedless English cucumbers sliced into ¼-inch (6 mm) medallions

MAKES ABOUT 1½ QUARTS (1.4 L)

SPICY CUCUMBER PICKLES

INSTRUCTIONS

1. Combine the water, vinegar, sugar, chiles, hot sauce, onion, garlic, fresh dill, salt, paprika, and dill seeds in a large nonreactive saucepan and bring to a boil. Remove from heat, allow to cool to room temperature, and refrigerate overnight.

2. Once the brine has rested for 24 hours, allowing flavors to marry, strain the brine through a fine-mesh chinois or strainer, discarding the solids.

3. Pack the cucumbers in a large glass jar and pour the brine over. Press plastic wrap down over the cucumbers to ensure they are fully covered with liquid. Store in your refrigerator for at least 5 days to allow the pickling process to complete before using the pickles.

3¾ cups (1.2 L) white vinegar

2 cups (470 ml) water

5 tablespoons (65 g) sugar

4 garlic cloves, smashed

2 tablespoons plus 2 teaspoons (50 g) kosher salt

2 tablespoons (10 g) whole black peppercorns

1 tablespoon (11 g) yellow mustard seeds

5 fronds dill

3 seedless English cucumbers, sliced into ¼-inch (6 mm) medallions

**MAKES ABOUT
2 QUARTS (1.9 L)**

DILL PICKLES

INSTRUCTIONS ———————

1. Combine the vinegar, water, sugar, garlic, salt, peppercorns, and mustard seeds in a medium nonreactive saucepan and bring to a boil. Remove from the heat and allow to cool to room temperature, then add the dill. Allow the brine to rest in your refrigerator for 24 hours.

2. The next day, strain the brine through a fine-mesh chinois or strainer and discard the solids. Pack the cucumbers in a 1-quart (946 ml) glass jar and pour in the strained liquid. Cover with plastic wrap, gently pressing the wrap down on top to make sure everything is submerged.

3. Store in your refrigerator for at least 5 days to allow the pickling process to complete.

   Note: It is very important to add the dill once the brine is cool and to let the brine rest for a day to preserve the fresh dill flavor. When dill is heated, its taste changes completely. Also, there's no hurry up and wait with this one. Take your time. Taste the brine and adjust it to your preference. Enjoy after the cucumbers take their cool, 5-day rest in the brine.

2 **pounds (910 g)** Kirby cucumbers
(or pickling cucumbers), sliced into
¼-inch (6 mm) medallions

1 **medium** yellow onion, julienned

3¼ **cups (764 ml)** water

2¼ **cups (529 ml)** apple cider vinegar

1 **cup (200 g)** white sugar

1 **cup (225 g)** packed light brown sugar

2 **tablespoons (38 g)** kosher salt

2½ **teaspoons (9 g)**
yellow mustard seeds

2½ **teaspoons (5 g)** celery seeds

½ **teaspoon** ground turmeric

**MAKES ABOUT
2 QUARTS (1.9 L)**

BREAD AND BUTTER PICKLES

INSTRUCTIONS ——————

1. Combine the sliced cucumbers and onion in a heat proof vessel.

2. Combine the water, vinegar, white sugar, brown sugar, salt, mustard seeds, celery seeds, and turmeric in a medium nonreactive saucepan. Bring to a boil over medium-high heat to make a brine. Pour the boiling hot brine over the cucumbers and onion. Allow to cool to room temperature. Cover with plastic wrap, gently pressing the wrap down on top to make sure everything is submerged.

3. Transfer the cukes and onion to a large glass jar and pour in the brine to cover. Cover and refrigerate for 5 days to allow the pickling process to complete.

Pickled Fresno Chiles

6 garlic cloves, smashed

½ cup (50 g) peeled and thinly sliced (across the grain) fresh ginger

1½ cups (353 ml) apple cider vinegar

1 cup (235 ml) water

½ cup plus 1 tablespoon (240 g) packed light brown sugar

1 tablespoon plus 1 teaspoon (25 g) kosher salt

2 pounds (910 g) Fresno chiles, stemmed and sliced into ¼-inch (6 mm) rings

MAKES ABOUT 1½ QUARTS (1.4 L)

Sliced into rings or later chopped into relishes, these fiery beauties add not only heat, but a vibrant fire-engine-red accent to the plates they adorn. Give yourself the gift of heat all year round by keeping a jar of these in your refrigerator. Serve on cheese or charcuterie boards or on your favorite sandwich.

INSTRUCTIONS ——————

1. Make a sachet by wrapping the garlic and ginger in a square of cheesecloth and tying it up with butcher's twine. Place the sachet in a large stockpot (or see Note below). Add the vinegar, water, brown sugar, and salt and bring to a boil. Stir until the brown sugar and salt dissolve.

2. Remove the pan from the heat and allow to cool to room temperature. Discard the sachet. Pack the chiles in a large glass jar and pour the brine over. Cover with plastic wrap, gently pressing the wrap down on top to make sure everything is submerged.

3. Store in your refrigerator for at least 3 days prior to serving to allow the pickling process to complete.

Note: If you don't want to make a sachet, add the garlic and ginger directly to the brine and strain the brine through a fine-mesh chinois or strainer before pouring over the chiles.

Pickled Green Tomatoes

⅓ cup (27 g) whole black peppercorns

1 (5-inch/13-cm long) thumb
fresh ginger, peeled and cut into
¼-inch (6 mm) medallions

2 tablespoons (10 g) coriander seeds

2 bay leaves

5 pounds (2.3 kg) green tomatoes,
sliced ¼ inch (6 mm) thick

1¾ cups (411 ml) water

1 cup (235 ml) white vinegar

1 cup (200 g) sugar

¼ cup (75 g) kosher salt

**MAKES ABOUT
2 QUARTS (1.9 L)**

Everyone who plants tomatoes knows that you always end up with too many tomatoes. One of the ways to cull the herd, so to speak, is to pick a lot of them while they are still green and get them in a pickling brine. Pickled green tomatoes are a strong presence in African American foodways and are a great building block for all kinds of relishes and salsas.

INSTRUCTIONS ——————

1. Make a sachet by placing the peppercorns, ginger, coriander, and bay leaves in a square of cheesecloth and tying it up with butcher's twine (or see Note below). Put the green tomatoes in a large container with an airtight lid.

2. Combine the water, vinegar, sugar, salt, and sachet in a large nonreactive saucepan and bring to a boil, stirring to dissolve the sugar and salt. Remove the brine from the heat, discard the sachet, and allow to cool to room temperature.

3. Pour the cooled brine over the tomatoes. Cover with plastic wrap, gently pressing the wrap down on top to make sure everything is submerged. Store in the refrigerator for at least 2 days before serving to allow the pickling process to complete.

Note: If you don't want to make a sachet, add the peppercorns, ginger, coriander, and bay leaves directly to the brine and strain the brine through a fine-mesh chinois or strainer before pouring over the tomatoes.

Pickled Okra

1½ cups (353 ml) rice vinegar

½ cup (118 ml) apple cider vinegar

¾ cup (150 g) sugar

1¼ cups (294 ml) water

2 garlic cloves, smashed

1 (2-inch) thumb fresh ginger, peeled
and sliced into ¼-inch medallions

3 chiles de árbol

2 tablespoons plus 2 teaspoons
(50 g) kosher salt

1 star anise

4 allspice berries

1 whole black peppercorn

1 teaspoon coriander seeds

4 cups (400 g) sliced okra
(½-inch/1 cm rings)

**MAKES ABOUT
1½ QUARTS (1.4 L)**

Like all kinds of cucumber pickles, pickled okra can be found on the condiment shelves of any grocery store, ready for you to take home for your house party. But doing that would be denying yourself the unique, aromatic flavor of the spices in this brine—the star anise, allspice, and coriander bringing an element of Southeast Asian cuisine to traditional soul food flavors.

INSTRUCTIONS ——————————

1. Combine the rice vinegar, cider vinegar, sugar, water, garlic, ginger, chiles, salt, star anise, allspice, peppercorn, and coriander in a medium nonreactive saucepan and bring to a boil. Reduce to a simmer and cook for 10 minutes. Remove from the heat and allow to cool to room temperature.

2. Put the okra in a large glass jar and pour the cooled brine over the okra. Cover with plastic wrap, gently pressing the film down on top to make sure everything is submerged.

3. Store in your refrigerator for at least 2 days before using to allow the pickling process to complete.

"PATIENCE, GRASSHOPPER," OR, IT'LL BE READY WHEN IT'S DONE

Your friend and mine, Chef Tom Colicchio, is famous for telling people, when they ask him how long to cook something, "Until it's done." I'll offer a similar take when it comes to pickling and preserving. Most of the recipes in this chapter require at least a few days—if not a week—in the refrigerator for the flavors and textures to arrive at the best end result. Initially the heat from the pickle brine allows its flavors to penetrate and lightly cook the vegetables, but as the ingredients cool down, the vegetables begin to release their flavors into the brine and reabsorb them. The process needs to run its course and can't be rushed, so be patient. After a few days, you'll have made a delicious, versatile ingredient that will last you a lot longer than you had to wait.

Pickled Peaches

3 cups (705 ml) champagne vinegar

½ cup (118 ml) red wine vinegar

1 cup (235 ml) water

2 cups (400 g) sugar

1 (1-inch/2.5 cm) stick cinnamon

¼ star anise

2 allspice berries

¾ teaspoon whole black peppercorns

1 small sprig fresh rosemary

1 teaspoon juniper berries

2½ pounds (1.1 kg) peaches, pitted and cut it into eighths

**MAKES ABOUT
2 QUARTS (1.9 L)**

Nothing reminds me more of my early years in Atlanta than my introduction to pickled Georgia peaches. These flavors scream Southern cooking and soul food to me. A perfect example of a delicate fruit being given an extended life beyond its short growing season.

INSTRUCTIONS ───────────

1. Combine the champagne and red wine vinegars, water, and sugar in a large nonreactive saucepan and bring to a boil. Add the cinnamon, anise, allspice berries, peppercorns, rosemary, and juniper berries. Remove from the heat and allow the pickling liquid to cool to room temperature. Refrigerate until cold.

2. Pour the cooled pickling liquid over the peaches in a large glass jar, ensuring that the fruit is completely covered in liquid. Cover with plastic wrap, gently pressing the wrap down on top to make sure everything is submerged. Allow to brine for a minimum of 5 days in your refrigerator to allow the pickling process to complete before serving.

Pickled Pears

5 **pounds (2.3 kg)** Bosc pears

2½ **cups (588 ml)** water

1¼ **cups (294 ml)** white balsamic vinegar

1¾ **cups (350 g)** sugar

¾ **cup (255 g)** honey

½ **cup (150 g)** kosher salt

2½ **tablespoons (13 g)** whole black peppercorns

2 **sprigs** fresh thyme

2 **sprigs** fresh mint

**MAKES ABOUT
3 QUARTS (2.8 L)**

The best time to pickle pears is early in their season, when the pears are firm and a little bland. This allows you to really kick them into high gear with the aromatic flavors of this pickling brine. Keep these around for cocktail garnishes or serve them with a chilled bucket of craft cider.

INSTRUCTIONS ────────────

1. Slice the pears in half lengthwise, remove the stems and cores and cut each half into slices lengthwise. Place the sliced pears in a heatproof, nonreactive container.

2. Combine the water, vinegar, sugar, honey, salt, peppercorns, thyme, and mint in a nonreactive saucepan and bring to a boil. Remove from the heat and pour over the pears. Cover with plastic wrap, gently pressing the wrap down on top to make sure everything is submerged. Allow to cool to room temperature. Store in the refrigerator for at least 3 days to allow the pickling process to complete.

Pickled Red Onions

2 cups (470 ml) white vinegar

⅔ cup (157 ml) red wine vinegar

1⅓ cups (313 ml) water

⅓ cup (67 g) sugar

2 allspice berries

½ star anise

1 teaspoon whole black peppercorns

½ teaspoon kosher salt

10 cups (1.6 kg) peeled and
julienned red onions

**MAKES ABOUT
2 QUARTS (1.9 L)**

Pickled red onions are a perennial necessity in any restaurant kitchen, and I recommend them for the home refrigerator, too. Use them on salads, sandwiches, and burgers or alongside any kind of barbecue.

INSTRUCTIONS ─────────

1. Combine the white vinegar, red wine vinegar, water, sugar, allspice, star anise, peppercorns, and salt in a nonreactive saucepan. Place over medium heat, stirring constantly, until the sugar and salt are fully dissolved and the brine is aromatic. Remove from the heat and allow to cool to room temperature.

2. Pack the onions into a large glass jar and pour in the cooled brine. Cover with plastic wrap, gently pressing the wrap down on top to make sure everything is submerged. Store in the refrigerator for at least 2 days to allow the pickling process to complete before using.

Pickled Strawberries

1½ cups (353 ml)
white balsamic vinegar

⅔ cup (157 ml) water

3 tablespoons (60 g) honey

2 tablespoons (26 g) sugar

2 tablespoons (38 g) kosher salt

2 teaspoons whole black peppercorns

4 sprigs fresh tarragon

4 sprigs fresh thyme

12 fresh mint leaves

2 quarts (1.4 kg) strawberries,
hulled and halved

**MAKES ABOUT
2 QUARTS (1.9 L)**

S ounds counterintuitive, right? But how often do you get a perfectly ripe strawberry, especially north of Tennessee? These pickled strawberries are a truly versatile ingredient, great on salads, as a gin cocktail garnish, or served simply on vanilla ice cream. Give these your best shot. You won't be disappointed.

INSTRUCTIONS ——————————

1. Combine the vinegar, honey, sugar, salt, peppercorns, tarragon, thyme, water, and mint in a nonreactive saucepan and bring to a boil. Remove from the heat and allow to cool to room temperature.

2. Pack the strawberries in a large glass jar. Pour the cooled brine over the strawberries. Cover with plastic wrap, gently pressing the wrap down on top to make sure everything is submerged.

3. Store in the refrigerator and allow to pickle for at least 24 hours before using.

Giardiniera

10 **serrano chiles**, stemmed and halved lengthwise

8 **jalapeños**, stemmed and sliced into thin rings

3 **bell peppers** of assorted colors, stemmed, seeded, and thinly sliced

8 **celery** ribs, cut into ½-inch (1 cm) dice

2 **carrots**, sliced into medallions

1 **medium** yellow onion, cut into ½-inch (1 cm) dice

½ **medium** head cauliflower, cored and broken into bite-size florets

½ **cup (150 g)** kosher salt

5 **garlic cloves**, smashed

½ **cup (50 g)** pitted green olives

1 **(4-ounce/113 g) jar** diced pimientos, drained

1¼ **teaspoons** chopped fresh oregano

1 **cup (235 ml)** apple cider vinegar

1 **cup (235 ml)** extra virgin olive oil

1 **teaspoon** red pepper flakes

1 **teaspoon** freshly ground black pepper

½ **teaspoon** celery seeds

**MAKES ABOUT
2 QUARTS (1.9 L)**

Roughly translated from Italian, giardiniera means "from the garden" and is a spicy celebration of all the flavors associated with Mediterranean food. Loads of vegetables, fresh chiles, herbs, and olives are preserved in an apple cider brine and olive oil, then aged for about a week until the flavors really bloom. Pro tip: One of the best by-products of giardiniera is the brine. Drizzle it on salads or grilled vegetables as a spicy vinaigrette.

INSTRUCTIONS ───────────

1. Combine the serranos, jalapeños, bell peppers, celery, carrots, onion, cauliflower, and salt in a large bowl. Refrigerate overnight.

2. Add the garlic, olives, pimientos, and oregano to the chopped vegetables.

3. Whisk together the vinegar, oil, red pepper, black pepper, and celery seeds. Pour over the salted vegetables. Toss together thoroughly and allow to marinate in the refrigerator for 7 days to allow the flavors to deepen and marry. (The giardiniera is very good at 7 days, but it's best at around 14 days.)

Pickled Watermelon Rinds

4 cups (600 g) ¼-inch (6 mm)
watermelon rind slices
(see Note below)

2 cups (470 ml) apple cider vinegar

1 cup (235 ml) water

2 cups (400 g) sugar

1 tablespoon plus 2 teaspoons
(31 g) kosher salt

6 sprigs fresh fennel fronds

¼ cup (25 g) chopped fresh ginger

1 tablespoon (5 g) whole black
peppercorns

2 sprigs fresh thyme

**MAKES
1 QUART (946 ML)**

The oldest pickled watermelon recipe that I've been able to find in the English language was written in the mid-nineteenth century, but the tradition dates back much further than that. Although pickled watermelon doesn't appear on many American dinner tables outside of the South, it has a strong legacy in Scandinavia and northern Europe. It became a big part of soul food all over the United States during the Great Depression, in large part because of Patsy Randolph in Harlem. As the story goes, Ms. Randolph would collect all the watermelon rinds from the street market fruit vendors, pickle them in her home kitchen, and sell them to neighborhood diners and restaurants. Thank you, Patsy Randolph.

INSTRUCTIONS

1. Combine the rind slices, vinegar, water, sugar, salt, fennel, ginger, peppercorns, and thyme in a nonreactive saucepan and bring to a boil. Reduce the heat to a simmer and cook until the rind is tender, about 20 minutes. Remove from the heat and allow to cool to room temperature.

2. Transfer the watermelon rinds and their brine into a large glass jar. Store in your refrigerator. These can be served and eaten as soon as they are chilled.

Note: Prepare the watermelon rind by using a vegetable peeler to remove the dark green rind from the outside and scraping all of the red flesh of the fruit from the inside. What's left should be a very pale almost-white green rind that is quite tough and crunchy. Slice this remaining rind about ¼-inch (6 mm) thick. (Note: a food processor with a slicer attachment will make slicing the rind much easier.)

NORTHERN SOUL

APPETIZERS

3

My favorite kinds of parties are the ones where the groove starts slowly; the music is a mellow, steady beat with some upbeat old school in the mix, the lights aren't down too low, everyone is on their second drink, and the conversations and laughter are beginning to flow. That's the way I like to put together my appetizer spread. My approach to the first bites of the night is to introduce some comfort and happiness, getting everyone to let their guard down with something they recognize paired with an element they haven't had before. Make your appetizers the conversation starter and the inspiration for the evening.

Char-Broiled Oysters with BBQ Butter

12 shucked fresh raw oysters with the oyster meat resting in the bottom shell

¼ cup (55 g) room temperature BBQ Butter, page 61

MAKES 12 OYSTERS

In addition to the two ingredients listed in the recipe, you'll need a few things to make everything easy:

1. An apron you're proud to wear. I recommend aprons from Craftmade Aprons (www.craftmadeaprons.com).

2. A pair of long (10-inch to 14-inch [25 to 36 cm]), spring-loaded tongs

3. A tall, cold, fizzy refreshment of your choice

4. Oyster gloves and an oyster knife

5. A friend who knows how to quickly and safely shuck oysters

6. Bandages and Neosporin (medicated ointment) for the party guest with the empty bourbon glass who keeps shouting about if he got on the show he could "totally beat Bobby Flay"

INSTRUCTIONS

1. Fire up your grill, spreading the hot coals evenly across the bottom (or, for a gas grill, preheat to medium-high). Place the oysters in the open shell on the grill grate and place the cover back on the grill. Grill for about 5 to 8 minutes, until the oysters are hot and cooked through and the liquid inside the shell has mostly evaporated (they should appear moist but not wet).

2. Transfer to a serving plate, divide the butter equally among the cooked oysters, and serve hot.

8 tablespoons (112 g) unsalted
butter, at room temperature

2 teaspoons (11 g) roasted
garlic puree or garlic confit

1 garlic clove, minced

4 teaspoons (13 g) minced shallot

4 teaspoons (5 g) chopped
flat-leaf parsley leaves

2 teaspoons minced chives

1 teaspoon lemon zest

½ teaspoon kosher salt

½ teaspoon freshly ground black pepper

½ teaspoon smoked paprika

¼ teaspoon cayenne pepper

1 pinch dried thyme

**MAKES ABOUT
¾ CUP (165 G)**

BBQ BUTTER

INSTRUCTIONS ————————

1. Combine the butter, garlic puree, minced garlic clove, shallot, parsley, chives, lemon zest, salt, black pepper, paprika, cayenne, and thyme in a stand mixer fitted with a paddle or a food processor and process until the butter is well mixed and the flavorings are evenly distributed.

Pimiento Deviled Eggs

One dozen large eggs

2 ounces (57 g) drained jarred pimiento peppers

3 tablespoons (42 g) heavy mayonnaise, preferably Duke's Real Mayonnaise

3 tablespoons (54 g) kosher salt

1¾ teaspoons (5 g) smoked paprika

1 teaspoon hot sauce, preferably Cry Baby Craig's Hot Sauce

¾ teaspoon Bread and Butter Pickle brine, homemade (page 42), preferably, or store-bought

¼ teaspoon cayenne pepper

¼ teaspoon sugar

⅛ teaspoon white pepper, preferably freshly ground

1 tablespoon (5 g) chopped cooked bacon, from 1 strip of uncooked bacon

Minced fresh chives, for garnish

MAKES 24 DEVILED EGGS

It seems few people sit on the fence when it comes to deviled eggs. Either they light up your life or they steer you to the bowl of potato chips and tub of sour cream dip. I think they're delicious, if not craveable—particularly this recipe. The filling is supercharged with pickle brine, pimientos, bacon, and Cry Baby Craig's Hot Sauce—all of those flavors coming together to establish a raucous burst on the buffet table. Spending the time to create this mixture an hour or two ahead of time—or even the night before—will allow the flavors to bloom out and become more pronounced. That will give you the opportunity to taste it first and decide if you want to add more salt, sweetness, or a little kick from some extra hot sauce. For special occasions, level up to high roller status on the presentation and top each filled egg with a tiny dollop of caviar and a dusting of chopped chives.

INSTRUCTIONS

1. Put the eggs in a saucepan and cover with cold water. Cover the pan and bring to a boil over high heat. As soon as the water comes to a boil, remove from the heat and let stand for 10 minutes, then drain the hot water and cool the eggs under cold running water. The yolks will be set but not so much that they turn gray and bitter around the edges.

2. Carefully peel the cooled eggs (note: older eggs will peel easier than fresh ones). Cut each egg in half, carefully scoop out the yolks, and set the yolks aside. Rinse the egg whites under cold running water to clean them of any bits of shell or remaining bits of yolk, then set them aside to drain on a paper towel–lined plate.

3. Make the base: Combine the pimientos, mayonnaise, salt, paprika, hot sauce, pickle brine, cayenne, sugar, and white pepper in the bowl of a food processor. Process until smooth and fully combined, 30 to 60 seconds. Add in the yolks and process until you have a fully combined mixture that is smooth and creamy. Fold in the chopped bacon.

4. Transfer the deviled yolks to a piping bag. Arrange the egg white halves open side up on a platter. If the egg whites are rolling around, you can use a paring knife to cut a "foot" or a flat surface on the bottom of the egg white to help it balance. Pipe the deviled yolk mix into the egg whites, and chill in the refrigerator, covered loosely with plastic wrap, for at least 30 minutes. Garnish with chives and serve cold.

"OUT OF MANY WE ARE ONE"

There's no shame in making an entire meal out of appetizers. Anyone who has been to Spain knows that way of eating is part of daily life. I personally love going to parties where the only food is a well-tended buffet spread loaded with everything from oysters and deviled eggs to fried shrimp and tiny sausages on a stick. Just remember that when you go that route, the right kind of balance between hot and cold and meat, seafood, and vegetables is not only going to help please everyone, but will ease up on your efforts while entertaining, because a lot of the cold stuff can be made a day or two ahead of time and unveiled while you're putting finishing touches on the hot bites.

Hush Puppies

1½ cups (188 g) all-purpose flour

1½ cups (210 g) yellow cornmeal

3 tablespoons (39 g) sugar

1 tablespoon (7.5 g) Old Bay Seasoning

1½ teaspoons kosher salt

1½ teaspoons freshly
ground black pepper

¾ teaspoon baking soda

3 large eggs

1½ cups (353 ml) buttermilk

1½ cups (150 g) chopped raw,
peeled, and deveined shrimp

1½ cups (195 g) corn kernels

¾ cup (120 g) minced yellow onion

¾ cup (135 g) finely diced
roasted poblano peppers

1 teaspoon lemon zest

Peanut oil for deep-frying

Green Tomato Relish
(opposite), to serve

**MAKES ABOUT
12 HUSH PUPPIES**

There's a reason no Southern fish fry or oyster house is complete without a constantly replenished pile of hush puppies. Never mind the old story that they were thrown to the dogs to keep them from howling for their dinner at outdoor barbecues ("Hush, puppies!"). The reason to make them is that they are a superb filler—the perfect base layer for a long night of enjoying a good bourbon in good company.

INSTRUCTIONS

1. Combine the flour, cornmeal, sugar, Old Bay, salt, black pepper, and baking soda in a mixing bowl. Stir until fully combined. In a separate bowl, whisk together the eggs and buttermilk. Make a well in the center of the dry ingredients. Pour in the egg/buttermilk mixture and mix with a spoon until just combined—do *not* overmix. Gently fold in the shrimp, corn, onion, roasted poblanos, and lemon zest.

2. Line a sheet pan with parchment paper. Using a spoon or a portion scoop, portion out the hush puppy batter into balls about 1½ inches (3.8 cm) in diameter and arrange the balls on the sheet pan. Cover with plastic wrap and store in the refrigerator for at least 1 hour.

3. In a countertop deep-fryer or Dutch oven heat the oil to 375°F (190°C), for deep-frying. Line a platter with paper towels.

4. Working in batches, fry the hush puppies until golden brown on the outside and 180°F (82°C) on the inside, about 5 minutes. Allow the oil to come back up to temperature before adding the next batch. Drain the hush puppies on the paper towel–lined plate. Serve hot with the relish.

1 pound (455 g) green
tomatoes, chopped

1 Vidalia or other sweet onion, minced

1 (4-ounce/113 g) jar
pimiento peppers, drained

½ cup (100 g) white sugar

1 cup (236 ml) apple cider vinegar

¼ cup (60 ml) water

1½ teaspoons celery seeds

1 teaspoon red pepper flakes

1 teaspoon kosher salt

¼ teaspoon mustard powder

MAKES ABOUT
2 CUPS (490 G)

GREEN TOMATO RELISH

One of the things I most want to share with you in this cookbook is the adaptability and versatility of these recipes. Green tomato relish is a perfect dipping sauce not only for hush puppies but for just about anything else crispy, hot, and fried. It's a great example of how Southern cuisine can dress up food from any part of the country; it can reinvent your favorite turkey hoagie, or a last-minute chopped salad when Mom and Dad swing by, or the steak and French fries you're eating in your underwear while you spend the night with Netflix.

INSTRUCTIONS ───────────

1. Combine the tomatoes, onions, pimientos, sugar, vinegar, water, celery seeds, red pepper, salt, and mustard powder in a nonreactive saucepan and bring to a boil over high heat. Reduce the heat to a simmer and cook until the liquid is reduced by about two-thirds, and the mixture has the consistency of a jam, about 30 minutes.

2. Allow to cool to room temperature, then chill in the refrigerator for at least 30 minutes. Serve alongside the hush puppies, and store any leftovers in the refrigerator.

Pimiento Cheese Dip

1 cup (180 g) drained diced pimiento peppers (from about two 4-ounce/113 g jars)

1 cup (120 g) grated sharp cheddar

½ cup (115 g) cream cheese, at room temperature

½ cup (112 g) heavy mayonnaise, preferably Duke's Real Mayonnaise

¼ cup (34 g) diced Bread and Butter Pickles, page 42, or store-bought pickles

2 tablespoons (30 ml) brine from Bread and Butter Pickles (page 42) or other pickles

1 tablespoon (19 g) kosher salt

1 tablespoon (7 g) smoked paprika

½ tablespoon (8 ml) habanero hot sauce, preferably Cry Baby Craig's Hot Sauce

¼ teaspoon sugar

¼ teaspoon white pepper, preferably freshly-ground

Pinch of cayenne pepper

**MAKES ABOUT
3 CUPS (729 G)**

I've never really understood why Pimiento Cheese Dip has only really stayed a staple in the meal plans of folks south of the Ohio River. It seems to check all the boxes for the kinds of things we love on a North Country dinner party table: Shredded cheddar? Yep. Chopped sweet pickles? Sure. Cream cheese and paprika? Yah hey. Can you spread it on a cracker and eat a whole jar by yourself? You betchya. Maybe it's the cayenne and Louisiana-style hot sauce that turns folks away—which is odd. You'd think that in a place that's lucky to get three months of suntan weather, we'd take all the heat we can get.

INSTRUCTIONS ──────────────

1. Combine the pimientos, cheddar, cream cheese, mayonnaise, pickles, pickle brine, salt, paprika, hot sauce, sugar, white pepper, and cayenne in a bowl.

2. Stir together thoroughly. Allow to come to room temperature before serving and serve with your favorite crackers.

Shrimp Cocktail with Green Cocktail Sauce

SHRIMP

4 quarts (3.8 L) Seafood Boil Broth
(page 164)

2 pounds (910 g) raw 16/20-size shrimp,
heads off, peeled, and deveined

GREEN COCKTAIL SAUCE

1 pound (455 g) green tomatoes

**1 tablespoon plus 2 teaspoons
(25 g)** freshly grated horseradish root

2½ teaspoons (38 ml)
champagne vinegar

1¼ teaspoons habanero
hot sauce, preferably Cry Baby
Craig's Hot Sauce

1¼ teaspoons Worcestershire sauce

1¼ teaspoons fresh lime juice

1 garlic clove, minced

SERVES 4 TO 6

As I've mentioned before, if you're taking the time
to create a special, memorable occasion—to truly
entertain—serve a version of a classic that communicates
who you are and how you want to treat the people you
care about. I want to share food that gives people a new
experience, one that might change their perspective and
fuel their creativity. That's a gift new environments have
given me in the past and one that has become second nature
for me to pass along to the folks I want to feed. It's why
I'm so inspired by fashion, and why I'm so passionate about
every kind of music on the planet. It's also why cocktail
sauce doesn't have to be the same color as ketchup. This is
a delicious opportunity to let your mouth change your mind.

INSTRUCTIONS ————————

1. To cook the shrimp, bring the broth to a rolling boil in a stockpot.
   Add the shrimp and cook until the shrimp are pink and firm but
   not rubbery, about 3 minutes. Remove the shrimp from the broth
   with a spider strainer or slotted spoon and chill for at least 1 hour
   in the refrigerator.

2. To make the cocktail sauce, fire up the grill or preheat your broiler.
   Char the tomatoes until blackened and blistered on all sides.

3. Combine the charred tomatoes with the horseradish, vinegar, hot
   sauce, Worcestershire sauce, lime juice, and garlic clove in
   a blender or food processor and puree.

4. Serve the chilled shrimp with the cocktail sauce.

Spicy Boiled Peanuts

2 quarts (1.9 L) water, plus more
for topping off if needed

1 cup (235 ml) habanero hot sauce,
preferably Cry Baby Craig's Hot Sauce

½ cup (150 g) kosher salt

1 (4-inch/10 cm) thumb
fresh ginger, peeled

9 garlic cloves

1½ tablespoons (8 g) cayenne pepper

1½ tablespoons (10 g) whole
black peppercorns

1 tablespoon (5 g) coriander seeds

3 bay leaves

3 pounds (1.3 kg) raw peanuts in shell

SERVES 8 TO 12

Boiled peanuts are another one of those American cultural conundrums that never seemed to make it north of the Ohio River. Usually made seasonally during the harvest, boiled peanuts were new to me when I first tasted them at a campsite at Bonnaroo. A couple from Tennessee offered them up while we were drinking whiskey together. To put it mildly, I was nonplussed. It took me a long time to try them again, and despite the same results, I resolved to find a way to fall in love with them. This recipe is the fruit of that effort. Let's just say if you have enough time (it takes a while to properly boil raw peanuts) and a cup of Cry Baby Craig's Hot Sauce, deliciousness is inevitable.

INSTRUCTIONS ⎯⎯⎯⎯⎯⎯

1. Combine the water, hot sauce, salt, ginger, garlic, cayenne, peppercorns, coriander, and bay leaves in a large stockpot with a tight-fitting lid and bring to a boil. Add the peanuts, cover, and reduce the heat to low. Cover and simmer for 4 to 5 hours; after 4 hours, check for doneness by carefully removing a couple of peanuts from their shell and checking to see if they are tender and not at all crunchy. Continue cooking if the peanuts are still crunchy. If at any time during the cooking the water level sinks below the top of the peanuts, add more water.

2. Remove the pot from the heat and allow the peanuts to cool in the liquid, uncovered. Strain the peanuts out, discarding the cooking liquid and flavorings. Serve the peanuts in their shells.

The Minnesota State Fair, aka the Great Minnesota Get-Together, takes place for twelve days every late August through early September and is the US's largest state fair by daily attendance.

SIDES

A side should never be the spare tire or guest bedroom of the dinner spread. It should be like a painting, a coffee table sculpture, or The Dude's rug. Sides need to tie everything together, man, and, in the best cases, draw everyone in at some point and reveal that they stand out on their own. That said, like all the other rules of good taste, too much can be too much. Even if you're making an entire meal of side dishes—which, quite frankly, is the style of eating in the world's most interesting culinary cultures—it's easy to try and please everyone at the table, and the next thing you know it's a Northern Soul rendition of Thanksgiving Dinner on a Tuesday in April. In short, take your sides seriously, but don't let them take over the meal.

BBQ Beans

½ pound (225 g) thick-cut bacon

½ medium yellow onion, diced

3 garlic cloves, peeled

1 Fresno chile, stemmed

½ jalapeño, stemmed and sliced lengthwise

1½ cups (353 ml) Coca-Cola Classic

1½ cups (118 ml) bourbon

¾ cup (176 ml) veal demi-glace or fortified unsalted beef broth

1 (8-ounce/227 g) can crushed plum tomatoes with juice

1½ tablespoons (22 ml) hot sauce, Cry Baby Craig's Hot Sauce, or other habanero bottled hot sauce

3 tablespoons (33 g) whole-grain mustard

5 teaspoons (60 ml) red wine vinegar

5 tablespoons packed (60 g) light brown sugar

3 tablespoons (45 ml) pineapple juice

3 tablespoons (23 g) Cajun Seasoning (page 22)

1 (16-ounce/439 g) can black beans, rinsed and drained

1 (16-ounce/439 g) can red kidney beans, rinsed and drained

1 (16-ounce/439 g) can butter beans or lima beans, rinsed and drained

5 sprigs fresh thyme

1 sprig fresh oregano

¼ teaspoon chopped fresh rosemary

¼ teaspoon smoke powder, preferably, or ⅛ teaspoon liquid smoke

1¼ teaspoons freshly ground black pepper

1¼ teaspoons fresh lemon juice

Kosher salt

SERVES 12

If one of the reasons you've gone to the trouble of picking up this book is that you want to cook better barbecue, I'm not going to let you get away with dumping a can of (insert major-label conglomerate) baked beans, bringing them to a sloppy simmer on your stovetop, and presenting them in vintage crockery next to the brisket. To hell with that. You and your guests deserve to get down and dirty—and this fully loaded, hot, and slightly sweet mélange of legumes is an edible exercise in the slow burn. Take the time to make these right, and you'll build all kinds of good memories.

INSTRUCTIONS ——————————

1. Chop the bacon into small (⅛-inch/3 mm pieces). Combine the bacon and 2 tablespoons (30 ml) of water in a large, heavy saucepan or Dutch oven over low heat and cook, stirring occasionally, until all the water has evaporated and the bacon is cooking in its own fat. Add the onion and continue to cook until the onion is caramelized and the bacon is getting crispy, about 5 minutes.

2. Meanwhile, combine the garlic and Fresno and jalapeño chiles in a food processor and pulse until you have a coarse puree. Add to the caramelized onion and bacon mixture and turn the heat to medium-low. Cook until the garlic no longer has a sharp, raw smell, about 3 minutes. Then add the Coca-Cola, bourbon, veal demi-glace or beef broth, tomatoes, hot sauce, mustard, 1¼ cups (294 ml) water, red wine vinegar, brown sugar, pineapple juice, and Cajun Seasoning. Bring to a slow simmer and cook to marry the flavors, 10 to 15 minutes.

3. Add the beans, thyme, oregano, rosemary, smoke powder, and black pepper, and cook until the beans are very tender and you have a nice thick consistency, about 20 minutes more. Add the lemon juice and season to taste with kosher salt. Serve hot. Leftovers can be kept in the refrigerator for 2 weeks, or frozen for longer.

TASTE BUDS NEED TLC

Palate fatigue is a real thing—particularly when small plates and side dishes are the stars of the show. Be aware of the flavor profiles of everything you're serving and consider what it would taste like to have them all on your plate at the same time—which in fact is how you and most of your guests will eat them. Too many spicy and acidic dishes next to one another will make the sweet potatoes and mac 'n' cheese taste awfully bland, like yesterday's French fries. When your main courses are assertively flavored, greens are always a great bridge and a superb provider of both nutrition and balanced flavor.

Black-Eyed Peas

8 cups (1.9 L) unsalted chicken stock

2 cups (334 g) dried black-eyed peas

6 celery ribs, halved

2 medium yellow onions, halved

2 medium carrots, halved

2 jalapeños, stemmed and halved lengthwise to expose seeds

4 garlic cloves, crushed

20 sprigs fresh thyme

2 bay leaves

2 tablespoons (38 g) kosher salt, plus more as needed

6 ounces (168 g) chopped tasso ham, preferred, or ham hock

SERVES 6 TO 8

For a lot of us, black-eyed peas on New Year's Eve is a birthright, a foregone conclusion, tinged with bittersweet emotions. While the tradition honors our strength and resiliency, it's never lost on me that the first written mention of black-eyed peas growing in North America comes from the seventeenth century, when it was noted that my female African ancestors would hide them in their braids and head wraps, as they did with okra seeds, before being crammed into slave ships. Those who survived the journey planted them in the New World, a familiar and necessary nourishment—a reminder of freedom and home. Black-eyed peas are part of why I'm here. They are the flavor of triumph and perseverance. Black-eyed peas are an edible rendition of the Maya Angelou masterpiece poem "And Still I Rise."

INSTRUCTIONS ─────────────

1. Bring the chicken stock to a boil. Add the black-eyed peas, onions, carrots, jalapeños, garlic, thyme, bay leaves, salt, and ham. Bring to a simmer and cook over medium-low heat, partially covered, for about 1 hour, until the black-eyed peas are tender.

2. Taste the black-eyed peas and season them with more salt, if you like. Drain the peas, saving the broth for another purpose. Pick out and discard the onions, carrots, celery, and herbs (and, if you used a ham hock, the ham hock bone) and serve. The dish will keep for 2 weeks, covered, in the refrigerator.

Braised Chard

4 teaspoons (20 ml) vegetable oil

2 medium yellow onions, diced

4 garlic cloves, minced

2 bunches chard, stems removed, sliced into 1-inch-wide (2.5 cm) ribbons

⅓ cup (80 ml) fortified unsalted chicken stock

1½ cups (355 ml) water

1½ teaspoons kosher salt

¼ teaspoon freshly ground black pepper

1 pinch red pepper flakes

½ teaspoon apple cider vinegar

¾ teaspoon red wine vinegar

¼ teaspoon Worcestershre sauce

¾ teaspoon honey

1 pinch MSG

SERVES 6 TO 8

In the leafy green family, collards are the tough older sibling who keeps the house clean, makes sure you've done your homework, and puts all of their paper route money in a savings account. Kale is the middle child who pursues a bohemian life, wearing rope sandals and following traveling festival bands. Then there's chard, oh, sweet chard—the delicate, beautiful, youngest sibling who can paint like Matisse or perform in a metropolitan ballet by the age of nine. Chard is a lovely and resilient leafy garden green with a slight, clover-like, tangy flavor. While it can readily be sliced and added raw to green salads, it stands up to braising very well and doesn't take half the time to arrive at peak flavor and texture as its aforementioned siblings.

INSTRUCTIONS

1. Heat the oil over medium heat in a stockpot or Dutch oven. When the oil shimmers add the onions and garlic and cook until the onions are translucent, about 8 minutes. Add the chard, tossing with tongs to coat it in oil, and cook until all the chard has just wilted and turned a deep dark green, about 2 minutes.

2. Add the chicken stock, water, salt, pepper, red pepper, vinegars, Worcestershire sauce, honey, and MSG. Bring to a gentle simmer and cook, uncovered, until the chard leaves are tender, about 10 minutes. Taste to check for seasoning, adding more salt, MSG, or vinegar as desired. Serve immediately, or store in an airtight container in your refrigerator.

No Mayo Coleslaw

DRESSING

1½ cups (353 ml) apple cider vinegar

1 cup (235 ml) extra virgin olive oil

1 cup (200 g) sugar

3 tablespoons (42 g) bacon fat

1½ tablespoons (28.2 g) kosher salt

1 tablespoon (6.5 g) celery seeds

1 tablespoon (9 g) mustard powder

1½ tablespoons (9 g) freshly
ground black pepper

SLAW

2 cups (140 g) shredded green cabbage

1 cup (70 g) shredded red cabbage

1½ cups (16 g) shredded carrots

1 Vidalia or other sweet onion, julienned

SERVES 6 TO 8

The contempt and revulsion I hold for mayonnaise is no secret among people who know me or work with me. Its flavor, texture, and appearance make no sense to me. I avoid it at all costs. Maybe that's why I'm not seen at many church picnics. If I were to attend one, however, I'd bring a heaping bowl of this colorful, crunchy flavor rainbow and send Aunt Bonnie's creamy pile of cabbage packing—and I wouldn't feel bad about it.

The vegetables for the slaw can be cut 1 to 2 days ahead of time, but it is crucial the vegetables and the dressing not be mixed together until 1 hour prior to serving at most. This slaw should be crunchy; if it sits dressed too long, the vegetables will become soggy.

INSTRUCTIONS ————————

1. Combine the vinegar, oil, sugar, bacon fat, salt, celery seeds, mustard powder, and black pepper in a bowl and whisk together until smooth.

2. Toss together the green and red cabbages, carrots, and onion in a large bowl. Add the dressing, toss until the vegetables are evenly coated, and serve.

Buttermilk Biscuits

10 **tablespoons (140 g)** unsalted butter

3 **ounces (84 g)** lard or vegetable shortening

6 **cups (750 g)** all-purpose flour

¼ **cup (55 g)** baking powder

2 **tablespoons (38 g)** kosher salt

1 **tablespoon (14 g)** baking soda

3 **cups (705 ml)** cold buttermilk

½ **cup (24 g)** minced fresh chives

1 **cup (113 g)** shredded sharp cheddar

1 **cup (80 g)** cooked and chopped bacon, from about ½ pound (225 g) uncooked bacon

MAKES 8 TO 10 BISCUITS

To paraphrase Q-Tip: "Biscuits for my lunch, biscuits for my dinner, biscuits, biscuits, biscuits, makin' every meal a winner."

Biscuits as a slider bun for a fried chicken thigh and hot sauce—or for a three-bite BLT. Biscuits in the morning with honey butter or blackberry jam. How much sausage gravy do you have for a dozen biscuits? How about closing out dinner with a heap of ice-cold whipped cream and bourbon-slick strawberries on a pile of warm biscuits? Biscuits can be the meal, or they can round out the meal. They can begin or end your hardworking day. Biscuits are one of the first things I learned to make when I was young. They are a great meal prep to share with the little ones in your family because they are hands-on, require some gentleness, get better with lots of practice, and are the right amount of messy—like all of the best things in life.

INSTRUCTIONS —————————

1. Cut the butter and lard into pea-sized pieces and freeze in a covered container for about 30 minutes. Meanwhile, preheat your oven to 350° (177°C). Grease a baking sheet.

2. Sift together the flour, baking powder, salt, and baking soda in a large bowl. Using a pastry cutter or your fingertips, cut the butter and lard into the dry ingredients until the mixture has the consistency of coarse sand.

3. Make a well in the center of the bowl and pour in the buttermilk, chives, cheddar, and bacon. Using your hand or a wooden spoon stir together until a shaggy dough just comes together. Important: do not overwork the dough. Turn the dough out onto a lightly floured surface, dust the top with flour, and gently fold the dough over itself eight times

4. Flatten the dough into a 1½-inch (3.5 cm) thick rectangle and cut into 3-inch by 3-inch (7.5 by 7.5 cm) squares. Arrange the biscuits on the greased baking sheet at least 1 inch (2.5 cm) apart.

5. Bake for 15 to 20 minutes, until the tops are golden brown and the centers are cooked through. Serve warm.

Collard Greens

2 pounds (905 g) collard greens

2 medium yellow onions, diced

2 smoked ham hocks

5 garlic cloves, minced

9 cups (2.1 L) water

¼ cup (60 ml) white vinegar

4 teaspoons (16 g) sugar

1½ teaspoons kosher salt

2 teaspoons freshly ground
black pepper

2 teaspoons red pepper flakes

SERVES 6 TO 8

I don't think I take any vegetable as personally as I do collard greens. I know how they should taste and feel in my mouth. I yearn for the way they make me feel, how they augment and satisfy my appetite. I don't think I've ever savored a mouthful of collards and not thought about my ancestors. Collard greens are essentially the story of Southern African American foodways. A hearty green that could survive all kinds of weather with very little tending, collards could be left to grow while slaves and, later, sharecroppers spent every daylight hour laboring in the fields. The meager protein allowances of scraps and discards like pigs' feet, ears, and snouts went in the pot of shredded collard leaves with a dusting of salt and aromatics and were left to simmer for hours with a little splash of sugar and vinegar to cut the bitterness. While the adults were typically served the lion's share of the stewed greens and braised bits of protein in the belief that it was essential fuel for their labor, children were given the leftover broth to sip from cups and bowls. Modern studies have demonstrated that the salt added to the slow-cooking process draws out many of the nutrients like vitamin A, vitamin C, vitamin K, iron, and calcium from the greens, supercharging the broth. When I was a boy, hanging out in the kitchen with my grandmother, she would skim a cup of the collard liquor from the pot and hand it to me, telling me to drink up because it would "cure what ailed me." That kind of care, and her collards, are some of the best gifts she ever gave me. I've got an opportunity to carry forward all of that history, all of that care and work and generosity by sharing it with you in the pages of this book and in this recipe in particular. It's my way of moving forward. It's my way of making her proud.

INSTRUCTIONS ─────────────

1. Remove and discard the stems from the collard greens and chop the leaves into 1-inch (2.5 cm) wide ribbons. Combine the onions, ham hocks, garlic, and water in a stockpot. Bring to a boil and simmer, covered, until the meat is falling off the bone, about 2 hours.

2. Stir in the greens, vinegar, sugar, salt, black pepper, and red pepper. Cook until the greens are tender and silken, about 2 hours more. Serve warm.

Stewed Okra

⅔ **cup (150 g)** chopped bacon
(about 3 slices thick-cut bacon)

1 tablespoon (15 ml) water

½ **medium** Vidalia or other
sweet onion, diced

4 garlic cloves, thinly sliced

4 cups (400 g) fresh okra, sliced into
½-inch (6 mm) medallions

1 (28-ounce/794 g) can plum tomatoes,
drained and chopped

Kernels from **2 ears of corn**

1 cup (235 ml) unsalted chicken stock

3 tablespoons (45 ml) white wine

1 tablespoon plus 1 teaspoon (8 g)
freshly ground black pepper

1¼ teaspoons chopped fresh oregano

¾ teaspoon chopped fresh thyme

½ **teaspoon** red pepper flakes

½ **teaspoon** kosher salt

SERVES 6 TO 8

Throw away anything you think you might know about okra before you prepare this recipe. Served with rice, this dish can be a layered, fully loaded one-bowl meal, packed with nutrition, deliciousness, and all the best flavors of summertime. After you add the fresh herbs to the bacon and vegetables, your eyes will roll back in your head with a sort of spiritual ecstasy. I highly recommend serving this with a hot, fresh bowl of Carolina Gold rice and five or six portions of anything by Gary Clark Jr. played at a nearly excessive volume.

INSTRUCTIONS ────────────

1. Combine the bacon and water in a heavy pot or Dutch oven over low heat. Cook, stirring occasionally, until the water has evaporated off and the bacon has fried in its own grease, about 8 minutes. When the bacon is starting to crisp, add the onion and garlic and cook until the onion is translucent and the garlic starts to brown, about 8 minutes.

2. Add the okra, tomatoes, corn, stock, wine, black pepper, oregano, thyme, red pepper, and salt. Bring to a simmer and cook, uncovered, until the okra is tender and the flavors have all mingled, 30 to 40 minutes.

Cornbread Muffins

2 cups (250 g) all-purpose flour

¾ cup (105 g) cornmeal

1¼ cups (158 g) corn flour

⅔ teaspoon baking soda

1½ teaspoons salt

½ cup (112 g) unsalted butter, at room temperature

1⅓ cups (267 g) sugar

4 large eggs

2 cups (460 g) sour cream

MAKES 12 MUFFINS

The versatility of cornbread muffins allows them to cross into all kinds of daily meals. They can be a breakfast treat, crumbled and soaked in buttermilk; lunch with a little honey butter and slices of ham; or pulled just out of the oven and served with a pot of chili. If, on the rare occasion, they aren't all eaten the day they are made, dice them up and leave them out uncovered overnight, then give them a toasting in the oven. They make superb croutons in a salad.

INSTRUCTIONS ——————————

1. Preheat the oven to 350°F (177°C). Grease a 12-cup muffin tin or line with paper liners.

2. Sift together the all-purpose flour, cornmeal, corn flour, and baking soda.

3. In a stand mixer fitted with the paddle attachment, whip the butter until fluffy. Add the sugar and continue to whip until it is fully mixed in, scraping the sides of the bowl occasionally as needed. Add the eggs and beat on medium-low speed until combined. Add the dry ingredients in three equal batches until just combined, Then fold in the sour cream.

4. Fill each of the muffin liners two-thirds full and bake for 8 to 12 minutes, until the tops are golden brown and a toothpick inserted into the center comes out clean. Let stand for 10 minutes, then remove from the pan. Serve warm.

8 tablespoons (112 g) unsalted butter, at room temperature

¾ teaspoon cayenne pepper

3 tablespoons (60 g) honey

¾ teaspoon salt

**MAKES ABOUT
¾ CUP (165 G)**

HONEY CAYENNE BUTTER

This flavored butter is a cornerstone ingredient at Handsome Hog. Just a kiss of it pulls your taste buds into an edible roller coaster ride. Though I consider this a requisite with Cornbread Muffins, keep some around for all kinds of breakfast foods—and if you don't serve this with biscuits, we can't be friends.

INSTRUCTIONS ——————————

1. Combine the butter, cayenne, honey, and salt in a mixing bowl and use a rubber spatula to mix until fully combined.

2. Serve at once or store in an airtight container in your refrigerator. Serve at room temperature.

Creamed Corn

10 large ears of corn

1 tablespoon (14 g) bacon fat

1 large yellow onion, diced

1 teaspoon minced garlic

1 poblano chile, stemmed, seeds removed, and diced

½ cup (100 g) sugar

1⅔ cups (392 ml) heavy cream

¾ cup (180 ml) vegetable stock

1 tablespoon plus ½ teaspoon (22 g) kosher salt

1 tablespoon plus ¼ teaspoon (7 g) freshly ground black pepper

⅓ cup (42 g) corn flour

2½ teaspoons (11 g) unsalted butter

**MAKES ABOUT
6 TO 8 SERVINGS**

The presence of this recipe in this cookbook, as well as on the menu in my restaurant, is simply proof of my belief that if you're going to cook something almost everyone is familiar with, take that action uptown.

INSTRUCTIONS ─────────────

1. Shuck the corn and slice the kernels off the cob and into a bowl, taking care not to cut into the woody interior of the corn cob. When the kernels have all been removed, use the spine of your knife to scrape the cobs again, "milking" the cob. Mix this "milk" together with the cut kernel corn and set aside.

2. Heat the bacon fat in a stockpot or Dutch oven over medium heat. Add the onion, garlic, and poblano. Sweat over medium heat until the onion becomes translucent but does not color, about 8 minutes.

3. Add the corn with its corn milk, and the sugar, cream, stock, salt, and pepper. Whisk in the corn flour. Bring to a simmer and simmer for 15 minutes. Turn off the heat and stir in the butter immediately before serving.

Cucumber Salad

¼ cup (60 ml) water

¼ cup (60 ml) white vinegar

¼ cup (50 g) sugar

1½ teaspoons kosher salt

1½ teaspoons red pepper flakes

1½ teaspoons freshly ground
black pepper

2 seedless English cucumbers,
sliced into ¼-inch medallions

½ cup (75 g) halved grape tomatoes

½ Vidalia or other
sweet onion, julienned

SERVES 4 TO 6

This preparation, also known as Thunder and Lightning Salad because traditionally the ingredients were hurriedly plucked from the vines in the garden to prevent them from being damaged and lost when summer storms blew in, is a must for all warm-weather gatherings. The key to this dish is making the dressing about 48 hours in advance and then tossing everything together right away so the flavors of the ingredients have time to bloom.

INSTRUCTIONS ─────────

1. Combine the water, white vinegar, sugar, salt, red pepper, and black pepper, and store in an airtight container for at least 12 hours in the refrigerator.

2. Combine the cucumbers, tomatoes, and onion in a salad bowl. About 48 hours before serving, pour the dressing over and toss to combine.

Sweet Potato Mash

2 pounds (905 g) russet potatoes, peeled and cut into 1-inch (2.5 cm) cubes

1 pound (455 g) sweet potatoes, peeled and cut into 1-inch (2.5 cm) cubes

2 garlic cloves, peeled and smashed

1 medium shallot, julienned

1 sprig fresh thyme

¾ cup (180 g) sour cream

½ cup (112 g) unsalted butter

Kosher salt

¼ teaspoon freshly ground black pepper

1 tablespoon (3 g) chopped fresh chives

SERVES 4 TO 6

This dish is a great representation of my Northern Soul. Sweet potatoes and russet potatoes simmered (*not boiled!*) in a pot with aromatics and fresh herbs, lightly mashed, and tossed with that unholy North Country combination of sour cream and butter. Leave the marshmallows to Ernie Hudson, Bill Murray, and those other two guys and serve this one at your next dinner involving a large roasted bird and a national holiday.

INSTRUCTIONS ——————

1. Combine the russet potatoes, sweet potatoes, garlic, shallot, and thyme in a pot and cover with 1 inch (2.5 cm) of cold water. Bring to a gentle simmer over medium-low heat. Cook until the potatoes are just tender, about 30 minutes. (Do *not* allow the water to boil, which will overcook the potatoes.) Strain off the liquid and remove the stem from the thyme.

2. Return the potatoes and thyme leaves to the pot. Add the sour cream and butter and mash until all of the ingredients are fully mixed but still a little chunky. Season to taste with the salt and pepper. Garnish with the chives and serve.

Crispy Brussels Sprouts
with Bacon Vinaigrette

2 pounds (905 g) brussels
sprouts, trimmed and halved

2 tablespoons (30 ml) vegetable oil

2 quarts (1.9 L) peanut oil, for frying

1½ cups (353 ml) Bacon
Vinaigrette, below

SERVES 4 TO 6

Brussels sprouts and bacon are like peanut butter and
jelly—born to be together and never disappointing.

INSTRUCTIONS ───────────

1. Preheat the oven to 350° (177°C).

2. Toss the brussels sprouts with the oil and arrange in a single layer
   on a baking sheet. Roast until the sprouts start to brown on the
   edges but are not fully cooked, about 12 minutes.

3. Heat the peanut oil in a large pot or Dutch oven to 375° (190°C).
   Add the brussels sprouts and fry, stirring constantly, until they are
   browned and crisp, 3 to 4 minutes. Remove the brussels sprouts
   and allow them to drain briefly on paper towels.

4. Toss the brussels sprouts with the vinaigrette and serve.

1 cup plus 1 tablespoon (255 ml)
extra virgin olive oil

¾ pound (340 g) bacon, chopped

2 garlic cloves, minced

1 medium shallot, minced

½ cup (120 ml) balsamic vinegar

½ cup (120 ml) apple cider vinegar

2 tablespoons (22 g) whole-grain
Dijon mustard

⅓ cup (75 g) packed light brown sugar

MAKES ABOUT
3 CUPS (705 ML)

BACON VINAIGRETTE

There's something about the North Country that impels us to
suffocate healthy, nutrient-rich green vegetables with smoked
animal proteins as a form of insulating our arteries against
the polar vortex. This recipe will prove that bacon vinaigrette
isn't just for the restaurants you take your grandmother to for
her birthday.

INSTRUCTIONS ───────────

1. Add the olive oil and bacon to a large, cold skillet. Render the
   bacon over medium-low heat, scraping the build-up off the
   skillet surface as you go. Once the bacon is crispy, after about
   10 minutes, add the garlic and shallot and cook until caramelized,
   8 to 10 minutes more.

2. Remove from the heat, stir in the vinegars, mustard, and brown
   sugar, and allow to cool. Transfer to an airtight container for
   storing in your refrigerator.

Whole Roasted Cauliflower

6 cups (1.4 L) water

1⅔ cups (392 ml) white wine

¼ cup (60 ml) extra virgin olive oil

2 tablespoons (38 g) kosher salt

2 tablespoons (30 ml) fresh lemon juice

2 tablespoons (28 g) unsalted butter

2 teaspoons (7 g) red pepper flakes

2 teaspoons sugar

1 bay leaf

2 garlic cloves, crushed

2 sprigs fresh thyme

1 cauliflower head, outer leaves removed

SERVES 4 TO 6

I once worked at a steak joint in Saint Paul where the chef told vegetarians that they were regarded "with benevolent amusement." "We love that you're here," he would say. "We just think it's funny." Anyone who loves someone with a plant-based diet will be proud to set this dish out on a table as an alternative to the brisket, barbecue ribs, and fried chicken you've labored to bring to a succulent end.

INSTRUCTIONS ────────────

1. Combine the water, wine, olive oil, salt, lemon juice, butter, red pepper, sugar, bay leaf, garlic, and thyme in a large stockpot and bring to a boil. Add the head of cauliflower, reduce the heat to a simmer, and simmer for about 30 minutes, until fork tender. Using a slotted spoon or spider strainer, carefully lift the head of cauliflower out of the pot and set it on a wire rack to cool.

2. Preheat the oven to 375°F (190°C).

3. Transfer the cauliflower to a sheet pan and roast for about 25 minutes, until the cauliflower starts browning on the outside. Transfer to a serving plate and serve, allowing the diners to cut off their own portions in whatever size they prefer.

Bourbon Gastrique

2 **cups (300 g)** packed light brown sugar

1 **cup (235 ml)** apple cider vinegar

1 **cup (235 ml)** bourbon

1 **tablespoon (15 g)** whole
black peppercorns

1 **star anise**

1 **tablespoon (5 g)** coriander seeds

**MAKES ABOUT
1 CUP (235 ML)**

For your friends and relatives who have chosen a plant-based diet, this tangy, aromatic plant-based sauce is a great dressing on Whole Roasted Cauliflower, opposite, and other vegetables—as well as most meats—and keeps for long periods of time stored at room temperature.

INSTRUCTIONS ─────────────

1. Combine the brown sugar, vinegar, bourbon, black peppercorns, star anise, and coriander in a nonreactive saucepan. Simmer over low heat until large, slow bubbles appear and the gastrique is thick and syrupy enough to coat the back of a spoon and has reduced by about half, about 45 minutes.

2. Strain through a fine-mesh chinois or strainer and let cool. Serve at room temperature. Leftovers can be stored in an airtight container in a cool, dark place.

Hot Mac 'n' Cheese

2 pounds (910 g) macaroni pasta

½ pound (225 g) unsalted butter

⅓ cup (42 g) all-purpose flour

4 cups (940 ml) whole milk

¾ teaspoon onion powder

¾ teaspoon black garlic powder, preferably, or garlic powder

1 teaspoon freshly ground black pepper

1⅔ pounds (758 g) shredded Velveeta cheese

2¼ cups (520 g) sour cream

2⅓ cups (525 g) cottage cheese

1½ teaspoons cayenne pepper

8 to 12 ounces (224 to 336 g) Hot Cheetos, crushed

SERVES 8 TO 10

There is probably no more polarizing a dish in traditional soul food culture than mac and cheese. Historically, it has been the cause of innumerable fistfights, insults, snubs, irreparable family rifts, and divorces. I offer my rendition as a way to heal all of the aforementioned: a delicious sort of peace treaty with crushed Hot Cheetos on top. If this recipe doesn't heal old wounds—or, worse yet, opens them up and causes new ones—just remember: You didn't get it from me. Note that we use richly flavored, mildly sweet black garlic powder when we make this at the restaurant, but you can substitute regular garlic powder if you cannot find the black variety. This recipe makes a big batch, because this is an excellent entrée when you are serving a crowd; you can, of course, reduce the quantities and make a smaller batch.

INSTRUCTIONS

1. Cook the macaroni according to the package directions.

2. To make the sauce: Slowly melt ¼ pound (113 g) of the butter in a large, heavy-bottomed pot over medium heat. Whisk in the flour, stirring frequently to make a golden roux. Slowly pour in the milk, stirring constantly until a smooth bechamel sauce has been achieved.

3. Add the onion powder, garlic powder, and black pepper. When the sauce comes to a simmer, add the Velveeta, one handful at a time, allowing each handful to melt into the sauce before adding more.

4. Reduce the heat to low and stir in the sour cream and cottage cheese in a similar fashion, allowing each batch to melt into the sauce before adding more. When the sauce is smooth, remove it from the heat and stir in the remaining butter and the cayenne pepper.

5. Drain the cooked macaroni and divide it among individual bowls. Pour the sauce over the pasta, top with about 1 ounce (28 g) of Cheetos, and serve.

Soups & Salads

5

In a lot of fine-dining kitchens, job applicants have to be willing to audition for the job—literally. Many chefs will sit a young cook down to an interview, ask a few questions about background and experience, then explain the philosophy of their kitchen's food and style of teamwork. They will then ask the applicant when they can arrive for a *stage* (rhymes with *mirage*)—an unpaid shift that functions as an audition or tryout. There's usually a simple or fundamental task assigned during the shift that is supposed to assess the cook's level of competence. Some of my friends who run kitchens ask their new cooks to sear a piece of fresh fish or season and grill a steak to a specific temperature. A lot of old-school French guys will order a new cook to simply poach an egg or make an omelet.

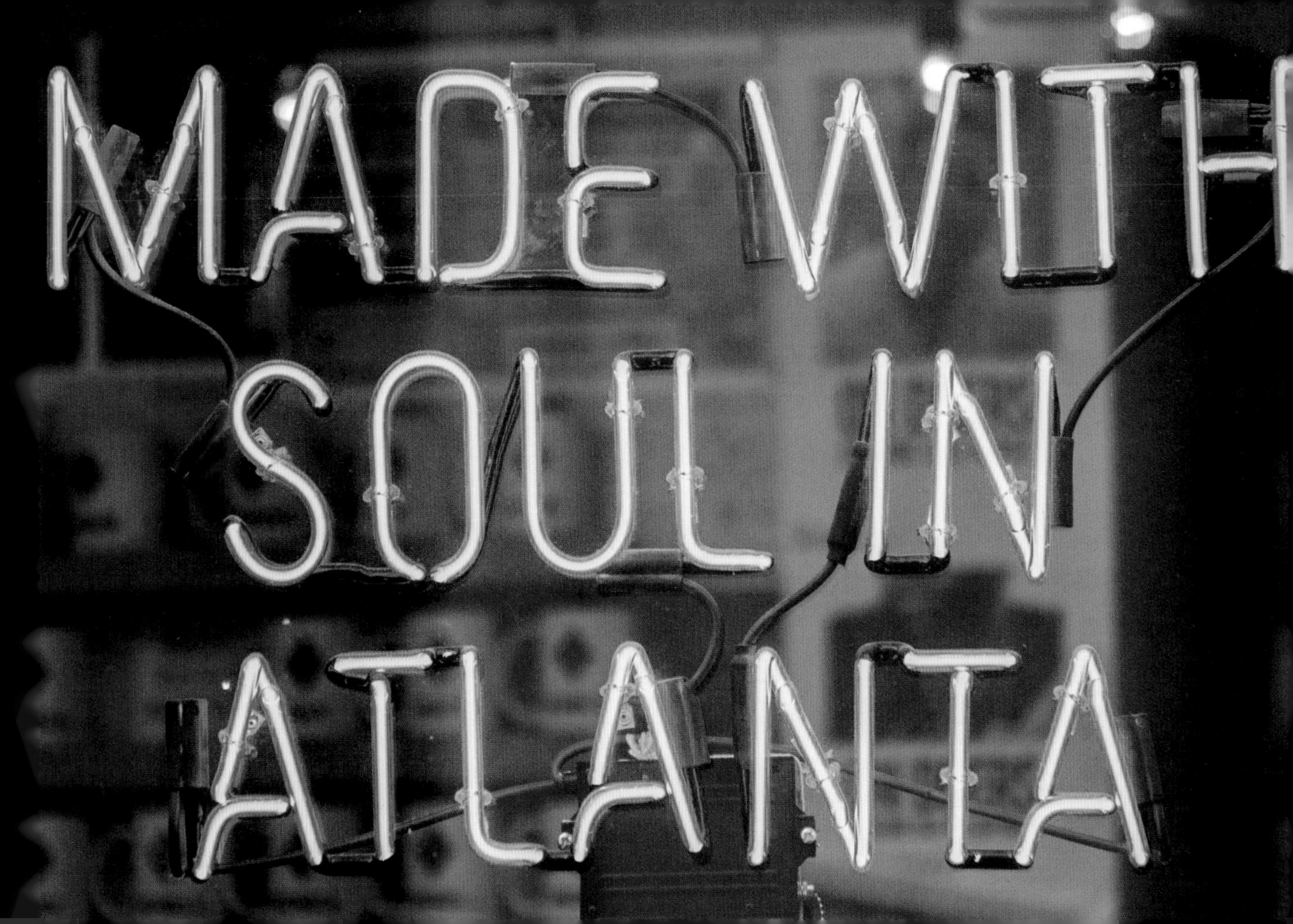
MADE WITH
SOUL IN
ATLANTA

Buttermilk Ranch Dressing

1½ cups (353 ml) buttermilk

1 cup (230 g) sour cream

½ cup (113 g) heavy mayonnaise, such as Duke's Real Mayonnaise

2 garlic cloves, minced

1 medium shallot, minced

1 teaspoon Dijon mustard

2 teaspoons dried tarragon

2 teaspoons dried dill

2 teaspoons dried parsley

2 teaspoons dried chives

1 tablespoon (6 g) freshly ground black pepper

1 teaspoon bottled habanero hot sauce, such as Cry Baby Craig's Hot Sauce

2 teaspoons fresh lemon juice

**MAKES ABOUT
3 CUPS (705 ML)**

Classics are classic for a reason, and they are the stuff of our childhood memories. This rendition of ranch dressing aims to capture a childhood memory of mine, and perhaps even improve upon it. As simple as its approach is, this recipe requires a bit of finesse and careful timing. In order for the flavors, particularly of the dried herbs, to layer properly, they need an overnight soak to steep like tea and come to life. Make this a day or two before serving.

INSTRUCTIONS ————————

1. Whisk together the buttermilk, sour cream, mayonnaise, garlic, shallot, mustard, tarragon, dill, parsley, chives, pepper, hot sauce, and lemon juice in a mixing bowl.

2. Transfer to an airtight container and store in your refrigerator for at least 1 day before using to allow the flavors to marry. Store leftovers in the refrigerator.

BBQ Chopped Salad

2 corn cobs

1 **head** romaine lettuce, chopped

1 **cup (171 g)** black-Eyed Peas, see recipe, (page 76)

2 **cups (180 g)** shredded red cabbage

12 **grape tomatoes**

½ **cup (118 ml)** Buttermilk Ranch Dressing (page 101)

1 **(4-ounce/113 g) jar** diced pimientos, drained

1 **cup (30 g)** cornbread croutons (see Note below)

¼ **cup (34 g)** Pickled Red Onions (page 52)

1 **cup (140 g)** chopped leftover barbecued meat, such as pork, chicken, or beef

SERVES 4

Sometimes a grown-ass cook just wants a salad, damn it. Life is about versatility. And as often as our hunger demands curly fries and a drive-thru roast beef sandwich, it's important for us to check in every once in a while with our beautiful bodies and treat them to a bowl of fresh crunchy greens loaded with the kinds of treats we usually find on the backyard barbecue spread. This salad is as versatile as I like my life to be—it's perfect for a light summer supper, boxed for a lunch break during a boardroom meeting, or stabbed at and savored lazily while rocking a long afternoon in a hammock at the beach.

INSTRUCTIONS ——————————

1. Grill the 2 corn cobs over a medium fire for about 4 minutes per side. Remove from the heat, let cool slightly, and cut the kernels from the cobs. Set aside.

2. Toss together the lettuce, black-eyed peas, cabbage, half the corn, and half the tomatoes in a large bowl. Add the dressing and toss again.

3. Divide the salad equally among four bowls, then garnish each bowl with the remaining corn and tomatoes, the pimientos, croutons, pickled onions, and meat.

   Note: You can make your own cornbread croutons from leftover cornbread or cornbread muffins (page 84). When the cornbread is just starting to go stale, slice it into cubes, lay the cubes in a single layer on a baking sheet, and toast in a 175° (79°C) oven for about 25 minutes, until the cubes are dehydrated and crunchy, but not burned.

Watermelon Salad
with Bourbon Vinaigrette

1 medium watermelon, seeded and cut into 1-inch (2.5 cm) cubes

2 English cucumbers, seeded and cut into ½-inch (1 cm) slices

2 cups (40 g) baby arugula

¼ cup (35 g) sliced Pickled Fresno Chiles (page 44)

1 large shallot, cut horizontally into thin rings

¼ cup (25 g) toasted pecans

1 recipe Bourbon Vinaigrette, below

1 tablespoon (18 g) smoked salt

SERVES 6 TO 10

Nothing signals the arrival of summer like watermelon! This salad is a fresh way to enjoy this amazing fruit and will definitely make you the star of the BBQ. Just remember: If you swallow a seed, a watermelon might grow in your stomach!

INSTRUCTIONS ——————

1. Toss together the watermelon, cucumbers, arugula, chiles, shallot, and pecans in a salad bowl.

2. Toss the salad ingredients with the vinaigrette, sprinkle smoked salt over the top, and serve.

---

1 cup (235 ml) bourbon

½ cup (176 g) Dijon mustard

2 tablespoons (22 g) whole-grain mustard

½ cup (118 ml) apple cider vinegar

¼ cup (40 g) minced shallots

2 tablespoons (26 g) sugar

1 tablespoon plus ¾ teaspoon (7 g) freshly ground black pepper

1½ teaspoons kosher salt

1 cup (235 ml) extra virgin olive oil

MAKES ABOUT
3 CUPS (705 ML)

BOURBON VINAIGRETTE

A delicate part of this recipe is igniting the bourbon to cook off the alcohol and enhance the deep, smoky flavors that make it so distinctive. Cook the reduction in a well-ventilated space and over a low flame to prevent any loose clothing, or, in my case, substantial facial hair, from catching fire. That will ruin any party.

INSTRUCTIONS ——————

1. Heat the bourbon in a saucepan over medium heat until the fumes ignite. Continue to cook over low heat, swirling constantly, until the flame dies out. Remove from the heat and allow to cool to room temperature.

2. Whisk together the bourbon, both mustards, vinegar, shallots, sugar, pepper, and salt in a large mixing bowl. Slowly drizzle the olive oil into the bowl while whisking vigorously to emulsify.

3. Serve immediately or store in an airtight container in your refrigerator. Allow to come to room temperature before using.

Southern Wedge Salad
with Green Goddess Dressing

1 recipe Green Goddess Dressing
(page 106)

1 large or 2 small heads iceberg
lettuce, cores removed; cut a large head
into 4 wedges, or the smaller heads
into 2 wedges each

2 medium ripe peaches,
pitted and diced

1 cup (180 g) halved grape tomatoes

¼ cup (55 g) crumbled cooked bacon

½ cup (60 g) Pickled Red Onions
(page 52)

¼ cup (45 g) Spicy Boiled Peanuts
(page 69)

3 tablespoons (9 g) minced fresh chives

½ cup (60 g) crumbled blue cheese

SERVES 4

There is nothing more quintessential at a Midwest supper club than the wedge salad. This recipe adds some Southern flair.

INSTRUCTIONS ───────

1. Pour a generous portion of the dressing onto the bottom of four salad plates. Place a lettuce wedge in the center of each plate. Pour some more dressing over the top of each wedge.

2. Evenly distribute all of the remaining ingredients on and around the lettuce wedges on each plate and serve.

2 ripe avocados

1½ cups (353 ml) buttermilk

2 tablespoons plus 2 teaspoons
(40 ml) champagne vinegar

2 whole peeled garlic cloves

1 shallot, roughly chopped

1 teaspoon sugar

¼ cup (16 g) chopped fresh
tarragon leaves

¼ cup (15 g) chopped fresh
flat-leaf parsley leaves

¼ cup (25 g) chopped
green parts only scallions

¼ cup (15 g) chopped
fresh cilantro leaves

2 teaspoons fresh lemon juice

2 tablespoons (38 g) kosher salt

1 teaspoon white pepper

¼ cup (60 ml) extra virgin olive oil

**MAKES ABOUT
3½ CUPS (1 L)**

GREEN GODDESS DRESSING

Everyone should have a jar of this Green Goddess Dressing in the fridge—it's the aromatic, piquant upgrade to all the grocery store salad dressings in your pantry that have long passed their expiration date. If Caesar salad dressing is Jay-Z, green goddess is Beyoncé.

INSTRUCTIONS ─────────────

1. Remove the pits from the avocados, scoop out the flesh, and put in a blender. Add the buttermilk, vinegar, garlic, shallot, sugar, tarragon, parsley, scallions, cilantro, lemon juice, salt, and white pepper. Start the blender on the lowest setting, then gradually increase the speed to the highest setting. Blend for 15 seconds more, until everything has blended together.

2. While the blender is still running, drizzle in the olive oil to emulsify the dressing.

3. Turn the blender off, taste to check for seasoning, and serve. Store leftovers in your refrigerator in an airtight container.

READ THE ROOM AND LOOK OUT THE WINDOW

In a sense, soups, stews, and salads are all one-pot meals. Once an ingredient goes in, it can't come out, so be sure to respect and care for all of your guests' dietary restrictions, allergies, or lifestyle choices. If you can't make a satisfactory vegan chili for twenty-eight people, it's a classy move to make two or three portions in a smaller pot for your cousin's new triathlete boyfriend—or RZA, who is strictly vegan, if he stops by.

Reading the weather is as important as reading the room. Make sure that you aren't serving chilled cucumber soup on a rainy day or gazpacho for Valentine's Day. Not only do you want to save a hearty stew for the week you need to warm your soul, but the kinds of ingredients that shine in chilled soups are usually only in season and taste best during the warm months of summer and early autumn. Patience, Grasshopper.

Crawfish Bisque

1 cup (225 g) unsalted butter

1 cup (125 g) all-purpose flour

2 Vidalia or other sweet onions,
coarsely chopped

2 red bell peppers, stems and seeds
removed, coarsely chopped

4 celery ribs, coarsely chopped

12 garlic cloves, smashed

8 plum tomatoes, cut in half

Chopped leaves from 16 sprigs
fresh thyme

2 cups (470 ml) dry sherry
or cooking sherry

3 quarts (2.8 L) seafood stock,
preferably, or vegetable stock

3 pounds (1.4 kg) crawfish tail meat

6 tablespoons (113 g) kosher salt

4 teaspoons (8 g) freshly
ground black pepper

2 teaspoons (4 g) cayenne pepper

2 cups (470 ml) heavy cream

6 tablespoons (90 ml) fresh lemon juice

¼ cup (60 ml) bottled habanero
hot sauce, such as Cry Baby
Craig's Hot Sauce

Fresh chives, optional, for garnish

MAKES 4 QUARTS (3.8 L)

My favorite afternoon lunch on a warm, rainy day. I'll put on a little Sidney Bechet, open the windows, and listen to the thunder rumble through the city. Saint Paul is a river town, a city of industry on the mighty Mississippi—a reminder, like this bisque—that New Orleans is never too far away.

INSTRUCTIONS ———————————

1. Melt the butter over medium heat in a large Dutch oven. When the foaming subsides, whisk in the flour and cook until you have an evenly mixed blonde roux. Add the onions, bell peppers, celery, and garlic. Cook, stirring occasionally, over medium-low heat until the onions are translucent, about 10 minutes.

2. Add the tomatoes and thyme and continue to cook, scraping the bottom of the pot continuously, until the tomatoes have released their liquid, about 8 minutes. Add the sherry and deglaze the pan, scraping the browned bits off the bottom. Add the stock, crawfish meat, salt, black pepper, and cayenne and bring to a boil over high heat.

3. Remove the soup from the heat and, working carefully and in batches, puree the soup in a blender, then pass it through a fine-mesh chinois or strainer. Return the pureed soup to the pot, add the cream, lemon juice, and hot sauce and bring to a boil one more time.

4. Immediately remove the soup from the heat, taste for seasoning, garnish with fresh chives if you like, then serve. Leftovers can be stored in your refrigerator in an airtight container.

Ham and Greens Soup

2 quarts (1.9 L) pork stock,
preferably, or vegetable stock

½ pound (228 g) collard greens,
stems removed and cut into 1-inch
(2.5 cm) wide ribbons

1 (14-ounce/396 g) can whole peeled
tomatoes in liquid

2 celery ribs, diced

1½ medium carrots, diced

1 medium yellow onion, diced

½ jalapeño, diced

½ garlic clove, minced

Chopped leaves from 2 sprigs
fresh thyme

1 bay leaf

6 tablespoons (90 ml) white vinegar

¾ cup (176 ml) chicken demi-glace,
preferably, or fortified chicken stock

¼ cup (60 ml) bottled habanero
hot sauce, such as Cry Baby
Craig's Hot Sauce

3½ teaspoons (18 g) light brown sugar

2½ teaspoons (20 g) MSG

1 teaspoon kosher salt

¾ teaspoon freshly ground black pepper

¾ pound (340 g) ham shank meat,
preferably, or ham hock or leftover
roasted ham, diced

**MAKES ABOUT
3 QUARTS (2.8 L)**

It's difficult to come up with a better example of the kind of rural, Southern one-pot meal that necessity turned into tradition. Scraps of ham left on the bone that was slipped in to simmering greens to give the broth some protein and personality provided a hearty, sweet, smoky flavor that paired perfectly with tart and bitter greens loaded with all kinds of nourishment. Be careful with the salt content on this one. Let the ham carry that heavy lifting so the greens can play their part and keep you and your guests coming back for more.

INSTRUCTIONS ─────────

1. Combine the stock, collard greens, tomatoes, celery, carrots, onion, jalapeño, garlic, thyme, bay leaf, white vinegar, demi-glace, hot sauce, brown sugar, MSG, salt, and pepper in a large stockpot or Dutch oven. Bring to a boil over medium-high heat, then reduce the heat to a simmer and cook until the greens are tender, about 50 minutes.

2. Stir the ham into the pot and simmer for another 15 minutes. Remove the soup from the heat, remove the bay leaf, taste to check for seasoning, then serve. Leftovers can be stored in your refrigerator in an airtight container.

She-Crab Soup

1 **medium** yellow onion, coarsely chopped

2 **celery ribs**, coarsely chopped

2 **garlic cloves**, coarsely chopped

¼ **cup (55 g)** unsalted butter

¼ **cup (31 g)** all-purpose flour

1½ **teaspoons** tomato paste

2 **tablespoons (30 ml)** dry sherry

2 **quarts (1.9 L)** half-and-half

2 **cups (470 ml)** heavy cream

1½ **teaspoons** Old Bay Seasoning

2 **teaspoons** Worcestershire sauce

1 **teaspoon** bottled habanero hot sauce, such as Cry Baby Craig's Hot Sauce

2 **tablespoons (8 g)** chopped fresh dill

3 **cups (705 ml)** shellfish stock, preferably, or seafood stock

1 pound (455 g) lump-crabmeat

**MAKES ABOUT
4 QUARTS (3.8 L)**

An elegant, silky South Carolina classic take on seafood bisque, she-crabs refer to the female of the species, which carry their eggs, or roe, several times a year and add a distinct flavor and texture to the preparation. However, female blue crabs are now protected by law, so modern preparations of this dish, like the one below, focus on a robust shellfish stock and lump crabmeat, which can be found in most grocery store seafood cases.

INSTRUCTIONS

1. Combine the onion, celery, and garlic in a food processor and process until reduced to a coarse puree.

2. Melt the butter in a Dutch oven over medium heat. When the foaming subsides, whisk in the flour and cook until you have an evenly mixed blonde roux. Add the tomato paste and toast it, stirring constantly, until the tomato paste darkens, roughly 2 minutes. Add the sherry and deglaze the pot, scraping up the browned bits.

3. Add the pureed vegetables, half-and-half, cream, Old Bay seasoning, Worcestershire sauce, hot sauce, dill, stock, and crabmeat and bring to a boil. Reduce the heat to a simmer and cook over medium-low heat, stirring occasionally, until the flavors of the soup have married together for about 30 minutes.

4. Remove the soup from the heat, taste to check for seasoning, and serve. Leftovers can be stored in your refrigerator in an airtight container.

SANDWICHES

I like sandwiches because after giving them the initial attention they deserve, they can eventually be eaten with one hand—leaving the other free to send a selfie to a jealous friend not having the same sandwich. I also love sandwiches because I love my life outside. Sandwiches can be made ahead of time, wrapped in paper or plastic wrap, and stacked like cordwood in the cooler I drag down the dock on my way to an afternoon of boating on the St. Croix River. Sandwiches can be piled high on a picnic table next to potato salad, say, or pickled okra, or green beans tossed in bourbon vinaigrette.

I think a lot of people forget that with a little dedication to sourcing, shopping, and prep, sandwiches can go upscale in a hurry. Almost every bakery makes a proper crusty, pillowy hoagie roll that you can order ahead of time. If your local grocery store or butcher shop doesn't carry tasso ham, an online search can have some of the best stuff in the world arrive at your door, sometimes already sliced. Get the good lettuce and tomatoes from your co-op or farmer's market. We've all had an unforgettable sandwich at some point in our lives. Give yourself up to the next chapter and become the person who can give your friends and loved ones a memorable, top-shelf sammie.

Carolina BBQ Sandwich

12 ounces (340 g) cooked
pulled pork shoulder, chopped

6 tablespoons (90 ml) North Carolina
Vinegar BBQ Sauce (page 28)

⅔ cup (47 g) No Mayo Coleslaw,
(page 79)

2 burger buns, halved

MAKES 2 SANDWICHES

THE
RECIPE FOR
**ROASTED PORK
SHOULDER**
IS ON
PAGE 138.

Like any other worthwhile craft, the hands-on preparation and timing it takes to produce unforgettable barbecue allows for a lot of tenderness and expression. Taking your time and putting love into your effort is only going to make the pork piled on these sandwiches taste better. Immerse yourself in the process and give yourself the time to do it right. Though one hour will get the job done, after massaging the rub into the pork shoulder, I highly recommend letting it rest in your fridge overnight. You'll taste the difference. Likewise, when the pork is finished and you remove the pot lid, allow it to cool at room temperature for an hour or so. The juices will permeate all of the meat and it will be that much easier, even with gloved hands, to pull it apart into manageable pieces that will soak up more sauce.

INSTRUCTIONS ─────────

1. If necessary, reheat the pork shoulder. Once it is hot, toss the pork shoulder with the barbecue sauce.

2. Pile the pork on the bottom buns, top with the coleslaw, and serve with the top halves of the buns.

Crispy Chicken Sandwich

2 boneless Fried Buttermilk Chicken (page 142)

6 tablespoons (120 g) Bourbon Bacon Jam (see opposite)

2 burger buns, halved

½ cup (50 g) Apple Celery Salad (see below)

MAKES 2 SANDWICHES

There's a reason nearly every fast-food drive-thru in America has a rendition of this on their menu. Salt, crunch, juiciness, umami, sweet, sour . . . it's all there. This recipe takes you to VIP-level flavor with a swipe of bacon jam and a tart and cool apple-celery slaw.

INSTRUCTIONS ────────

1. Line a plate with paper towels. Fry the chicken according to the recipe and allow to drain briefly on the paper towel–lined plate while assembling the rest of the sandwich.

2. Spread the bacon jam generously on both the top and the bottom halves of the buns. Pile the salad on the bottom bun, then add the fried chicken, and serve with the top halves of the buns.

---

2 tablespoons (22 g) Dijon mustard

3 tablespoons (45 ml) champagne vinegar

1¾ teaspoons sugar

1¾ teaspoons freshly ground black pepper

1½ teaspoons celery seeds

5 tablespoons (75 ml) extra virgin olive oil

3 green apples, cored and julienned

1 cup (90 g) thinly shaved fennel

¼ cup (40 g) thinly sliced Vidalia or other sweet onion

2 cups (120 g) celery leaves

MAKES ENOUGH FOR 6 TO 8 CHICKEN SANDWICHES

APPLE CELERY SALAD

Early on, I cut my teeth in the kitchen of a fancy French restaurant in Saint Paul, Minnesota, and I'm sure this recipe and its distinctive Normandy flavors are a vestige of that. The balanced flavors of the apples, celery, and fennel—all with their fresh, distinctive crunch—make it a superb accompaniment to fried chicken on this sandwich.

INSTRUCTIONS ────────

1. Combine the mustard, vinegar, sugar, black pepper, and celery seeds in a salad bowl and whisk until smooth. Drizzle in the olive oil while whisking continuously to emulsify the vinaigrette.

2. Just before serving, add the apple, fennel, onion, and celery leaves to the vinaigrette and toss gently.

1 pound (455 g) bacon

2 medium shallots, coarsely chopped

1 Vidalia or other sweet onion,
coarsely chopped

3 garlic cloves, minced

1 teaspoon chili powder

½ teaspoon smoked paprika

6 tablespoons (90 ml) bourbon

6 tablespoons (90 ml) pure
maple syrup

3 tablespoons (45 ml) balsamic vinegar

3 tablespoons (45 g) packed
brown sugar

½ teaspoon liquid smoke

**MAKES ABOUT 1½ CUPS (480 G),
ENOUGH FOR THESE SANDWICHES
WITH PLENTY LEFT OVER TO
USE ON SOMETHING ELSE**

BOURBON BACON JAM

**The booze in the bourbon will mellow during the cooking
process, leaving the smoky, vanilla flavors we all love about
my favorite sipping whiskey. Just the same, if you or any of your
guests are not comfortable adding it to the recipe, just leave it
out and let the bacon and aromatic spices share the spotlight.**

INSTRUCTIONS ——————————————

1. Cook the bacon in a Dutch oven or heavy cast-iron pan over
   medium heat until it is crisp and all the fat is rendered, about
   8 minutes. Remove the bacon from the pan and drain, leaving
   about ¼ cup (60 ml) of fat in the pan. Chop the bacon into small
   pieces and set aside.

2. Combine the shallots and onion in a food processor and process
   into a coarse puree. Add the puree to the Dutch oven and cook
   over medium-low heat, stirring occasionally, until the onions start
   to caramelize, about 20 minutes. Add the garlic and cook for
   1 minute more. Stir in the chili powder and paprika and toast
   until fragrant, about 30 seconds.

3. Add the bourbon and maple syrup and turn the heat to high,
   scraping the bottom of the pan to remove any stuck-on bits.
   Add the vinegar, liquid smoke, and brown sugar and bring to a
   boil, then reduce to a simmer. Return the bacon to the pan and
   continue to simmer until the sauce has a jammy consistency,
   about 10 minutes. Allow to cool to room temperature. Serve on the
   sandwich or store in an airtight container in your refrigerator.

Deviled Crawfish Roll

4 unsliced 6-inch (15 cm)
Italian hoagie rolls

1 recipe Deviled Crawfish Salad
(see opposite)

¼ cup (25 g) thinly sliced scallions

16 rings Pickled Watermelon Rinds
(page 56)

MAKES 4 SANDWICHES

As much as my time in a French fine-dining kitchen taught me to love the approach to cuisine, the crawfish roll is a situation where a grocery store baguette simply will not do. Get yourself a blonde, crispy-on-the-outside, spongy-on-the-inside, Italian-style hoagie roll. More than one. Get several. Get a pile going and stack these puppies like cordwood next to the beer tub and the BBQ chopped salad with buttermilk vinaigrette.

INSTRUCTIONS —————

1. Using a serrated knife, slice a V-shaped wedge into the top of each roll, making a deep trough for the salad filling.

2. Spoon the crawfish salad into the troughs, dividing the salad evenly.

3. Garnish each sandwich with the scallions and watermelon rinds.

ANOTHER REASON I GO LIGHT ON THE MAYO

Consider the weather when you choose a menu to prepare. If you're going to make a pile of sandwiches and allow them to fuel your fun in the sun, avoid the whipped white stuff in a jar and substitute a light vinaigrette or a simple splash of olive oil and vinegar. Mayonnaise, even when you take into account how heavily processed it is, doesn't react well to warm temperatures, particularly outdoors in the sun, for hours at a time. Don't let your po' boys be the reason you and your fellow yacht rockers spend two days fighting over who gets to use the loo and how often.

1 pound (455 g) cooked
crawfish tail meat

1 cup (225 g) heavy mayonnaise,
preferably Duke's Real Mayonnaise

½ medium yellow onion, finely diced

½ medium carrot, finely diced

1 celery rib, finely diced

3 hard-cooked eggs, diced

½ cup (72 g) stemmed, seeded, and
¼-inch (6 mm) diced Fresno chiles

1 tablespoon (3 g) minced fresh chives

1 tablespoon (15 ml) fresh lemon juice

¼ teaspoon garlic powder

1 tablespoon (11 g) whole-grain
Dijon mustard

1 tablespoon (15 ml) habanero
hot sauce, preferably Cry Baby
Craig's Hot Sauce

1 tablespoon (7.5 g) Old Bay Seasoning

1½ teaspoons (23 ml)
Worcestershire sauce

1½ teaspoons kosher salt

1 teaspoon Zatarain's
Crab Boil Seasoning

¼ teaspoon cayenne pepper

¼ teaspoon freshly ground black pepper

**MAKES ENOUGH FOR 3 TO 4
DEVILED CRAWFISH ROLLS,
DEPENDING ON THE SIZE
OF ROLLS YOU HAVE**

DEVILED CRAWFISH SALAD

Unless you live and play south of Baton Rouge, crawfish tails can be hard to come by. We're fortunate in Minnesota to have an embarrassment of riches when it comes to seafood purveyors and Southeast Asian grocery stores, where one-pound bags of frozen crawfish tails are easily procured. If that's not the case where you live, ask your local co-op or butcher shop if they can order some for you or jump online and find a site that will pack them in a case of dry ice and get them to your front door.

INSTRUCTIONS ─────────────

1. Drain and briefly rinse the crawfish tails under cold running water and allow to drain, gently squeezing excess liquid out of the meat.

2. Combine the mayonnaise, onion, carrot, celery, hard-cooked eggs, chiles, chives, lemon juice, garlic powder, mustard, hot sauce, Old Bay, Worcestershire sauce, salt, Zatarain's Crab Boil Seasoning, cayenne, and black pepper in a mixing bowl and fold in the tail meat. Taste for seasoning, then use in a sandwich. Leftovers can be stored in an airtight container in your refrigerator.

Handsome Hog Burger

2 (8-ounce/227 g) beef burger patties

¼ cup (53 g) Bourbon Onions (page 122)

4 slices bacon confit

4 slices pimiento cheese

¼ cup (58 g) South Carolina Mustard BBQ Sauce (page 35)

2 toasted burger buns

10 Bread and Butter Pickles (page 42)

MAKES 2 BURGERS

As I mentioned earlier, whether you're looking through my wardrobe, perusing my record collection, or taking inventory of my liquor cabinet, you'll arrive at the very obvious conclusion that subtlety is not my strongest personality trait. When it came time to create the hamburger that would define the first restaurant I opened as chef and owner, I knew we were pouring all of our chips on the table. It couldn't just be a bar burger. It had to be an experience, a commitment, a lifestyle choice. Most of all, it had to represent my soul. This burger, in all of its loud, messy, edible glory, is the story of my journey. And that journey's destination is you.

INSTRUCTIONS ————————————

1. Sear the burger patties in a cast-iron pan over medium-high heat on one side. Flip the burgers, top with the onions, then the bacon confit, and finally the cheese, allowing the cheese to melt while the burger finishes cooking to your desired temperature.

2. Spread the sauce on the tops and bottoms of the buns and layer the pickles on the top bun. On the bottom bun, rest the topping with the burger patty (itself topped with the bourbon onions, bacon, and cheese) and serve.

1 **tablespoon (14 g)** unsalted butter

1 **tablespoon (13 g)** bacon fat

2 medium Vidalia or other sweet onions, julienned

⅓ **cup (75 g)** packed light brown sugar

⅓ **cup (78 ml)** balsamic vinegar

⅓ **cup (78 ml)** bourbon

1½ **teaspoons** black peppercorns, freshly ground

1 **teaspoon** pure vanilla extract

¼ **teaspoon** liquid smoke

Kosher salt

**MAKES ABOUT
1½ CUPS (315 G)**

BOURBON ONIONS

Even if *you* don't like fried onions on your burger (in which case you're wrong), a good host offers them as an option. These are a tried-and-true staple whenever I'm entertaining.

INSTRUCTIONS ——————————————

1. Melt together the butter and bacon fat in a Dutch oven over medium-low heat. Stir in the onions and cook, stirring occasionally, until the onions are soft and caramelized with a rich brown color, about 25 minutes.

2. Stir in the brown sugar and allow the sugar to caramelize briefly, then add half of the vinegar. Cook until the liquid thickens to a syrupy consistency, about 8 minutes. Add the bourbon, remaining vinegar, black pepper, vanilla, and liquid smoke. Continue to cook until the liquid has reduced by half, about 10 minutes.

3. Remove from the heat and season to taste with salt. Allow to cool before serving. Store leftovers in your refrigerator in an airtight container.

2 cups **(450 g)** heavy mayonnaise, preferably Duke's Real Mayonnaise

½ cup **(188 ml)** habanero hot sauce, preferably Cry Baby Craig's Hot Sauce

¼ cup **(44 g)** whole-grain Dijon mustard

3 garlic cloves, minced

MAKES ABOUT 3 CUPS (694 G)

CRY BABY CRAIG'S AÎOLI

As I may have mentioned, I detest mayonnaise—and I love Craig Kaiser. My dear friend started his hot sauce business by selling fermented hot chile sauce made with locally grown, organic peppers directly to his friends' restaurants, Handsome Hog being one of the first. Today he's in dozens of grocery stores, co-ops, and boutiques, sells online by the gallon or the gross, and wants to put his hot sauce in your hands—or your pantry. I'll do my part to help him by sharing this recipe with you. It's the least I can do for a buddy doing his best to grow a longer beard than mine. https://crybabycraigs.com/shop

INSTRUCTIONS ———————

1. Stir together the mayonnaise, hot sauce, mustard, and garlic until fully combined. Serve immediately.

2. Store leftovers in an airtight container in your refrigerator.

Hot Brown

2 thick slices sourdough bread

8 ounces (225 g) sliced ham, warmed

4 strips cooked thick-cut bacon

½ cup (122 g) Mornay Sauce, warm (page 126)

¼ cup (30 g) shredded smoked Gouda cheese

2 teaspoons minced fresh chives

4 Roasted Tomatoes (page 126), to serve

2 fried eggs, optional

MAKES 2 SANDWICHES

The Brown Hotel is a long-standing facet of the jewel that is Louisville, Kentucky—a city I got to know well when I participated in Season 16 of Bravo TV's *Top Chef*. One of our toughest challenges involved cooking in the kitchen at the Brown Hotel—and not for a second did it leave my mind that a dish as representative of Southern cuisine as shrimp and grits or biscuits and gravy had been invented where I was sweating it out in an elimination round. Nothing about a Hot Brown is good for your blood pressure—nor, I might add, is a *Top Chef* elimination challenge.

INSTRUCTIONS ————————

1. Preheat the broiler in your oven with a rack about 8 inches (20 cm) from the heat source. Line a baking sheet with parchment paper.

2. Assemble the open-faced sandwiches on the baking sheet: bread on the bottom, topped with ham, then bacon. Pour the sauce over the sandwich, then sprinkle on the cheese.

3. Place under the broiler and broil until the sauce bubbles and the cheese has just started to brown on top, about 3 minutes. Garnish with chives and serve alongside the roasted tomatoes. Add a fried egg, if you're feeling naughty. (I always add the eggs.)

6 tablespoons (84 g) unsalted butter

2 tablespoons (26 g) bacon fat

6 tablespoons (47 g) all-purpose flour

2 cups (470 ml) whole milk, warmed

½ **medium** yellow onion, halved root to tip

½ **cup (60 g)** shredded smoked Gouda cheese

½ **teaspoon** kosher salt

¼ **teaspoon** white pepper, preferably freshly ground

1 **tablespoon (6 g)** freshly ground black pepper

Pinch of nutmeg, preferably freshly grated

**MAKES ABOUT
2½ CUPS (608 G)**

MORNAY SAUCE

You can't make Mornay sauce without first making béchamel—one of the five mother sauces in French cuisine, so learning how to make a Mornay is doubling down on your skill set. Additionally, Mornay sauce is a requisite ingredient on open-faced heart-attack sandwiches like the Hot Brown. Pour it on your next burger instead of adding a couple of slices of American cheese and tell your cardiologist I said, "Hey."

INSTRUCTIONS ————————

1. Melt the butter and bacon fat over medium heat in a medium saucepan. When the foaming subsides, whisk in the flour and cook, stirring constantly until the roux is blonde in color, about 5 minutes. Slowly whisk in the warmed milk.

2. When all the milk has been incorporated, add the onion and continue to cook until the sauce thickens and starts a low boil. Reduce the heat to a simmer and whisk in the cheese.

3. When the cheese is fully melted in and the sauce is a smooth, even consistency, turn off the heat, remove the onion, and season to taste with salt, white and black pepper, and nutmeg.

4. Remove from the heat and season to taste with salt. Allow to cool before serving. Store leftovers in your refrigerator in an airtight container.

8 plum tomatoes, halved lengthwise

2 tablespoons (30 ml) extra virgin olive oil

6 garlic cloves, minced

2 shallots, minced

2 teaspoons chopped fresh thyme

1 teaspoon kosher salt

½ teaspoon red pepper flakes

¼ teaspoon freshly ground black pepper

**MAKES ABOUT
3 CUPS (540 G)**

ROASTED TOMATOES

While these are necessary with the Hot Brown and on the Handsome Hog Burger, keeping a jar of these tomatoes on hand for a quick pasta preparation, some Spanish rice, or as an addition to a soup or stew makes for a good form of self-care.

INSTRUCTIONS ————————

1. Preheat the oven to 175°F (80°C). Line a baking sheet with parchment paper.

2. Toss the tomatoes with the oil, garlic, shallots, thyme, salt, red pepper, and black pepper in a bowl.

3. Arrange the tomatoes cut side up on the baking sheet. Roast until they collapse and are lightly browned, about 3 hours. Store in an airtight container in the refrigerator.

Pork Dip

There's gotta be an implicit agreement of intimacy involved with sitting down to eat a meal that's going to end up all over your hands and face. Choose your company wisely and keep a pile of napkins within easy reach.

(page 55)

PORK

12 ounces (340 g) pork loin roast

Kosher salt and freshly ground pepper

SANDWICH

4 cups (940 ml) unsalted chicken stock

2 hoagie rolls, split open

½ cup (120 ml) Giardiniera (page 55)

6 slices Swiss cheese

MAKES 2 SANDWICHES

INSTRUCTIONS ——————————

1. Preheat the oven to 375°F (190°C).

2. Season the pork generously with salt and black pepper. Place in a small roasting pan and roast to an internal temp of 140°F (60°C), about 45 minutes.

3. Remove the roasting pan from the oven. Place the meat on a separate plate under an aluminum foil tent to keep it warm. Over low heat, deglaze the roasting pan with the chicken stock and keep warm.

4. Slice the pork as thinly as possible. Dunk each slice in the stock for a few seconds.

5. Preheat the broiler in your oven with an oven rack 6 inches (15 cm) from the heat source. Line a baking sheet with parchment paper.

6. Lay the hoagie rolls on the baking sheet. Lay the pork loin in, then top with the giardiniera, then the cheese. Broil until the cheese is just melted, about 3 minutes.

7. Transfer the stock to two serving bowls. Serve with the sandwiches.

CREOLE MUSTARD

After preparing your first batch of this recipe, you'll never see sandwiches the same way again. Creole mustard is a necessary component of our Pork Dip Sandwich at Handsome Hog, but you'll start to use it on everything from sliced turkey on wheat to egg salad on a sourdough roll.

1 cup (235 ml) white vinegar

½ cup (118 ml) water

½ cup (88 g) yellow mustard seeds

4 garlic cloves, minced

1 cup plus 2 tablespoons (198 g) whole-grain mustard

¼ cup (44 g) Dijon mustard

¼ cup (85 g) honey

1 tablespoon (15 g) grated fresh horseradish

1 tablespoon (15 g) packed light brown sugar

1½ teaspoons kosher salt

¼ teaspoon cayenne pepper

MAKES ABOUT 1½ CUPS (264 G)

INSTRUCTIONS ——————————

1. Combine the vinegar, water, mustard seeds, and garlic. Bring to a boil, reduce the heat to a simmer, and cook, uncovered, for 30 minutes.

2. Whisk in the two mustards, honey, horseradish, brown sugar, salt, and cayenne. Remove from the heat and allow to cool to room temperature before using on the sandwiches. Store leftovers in your refrigerator in an airtight container.

Shrimp Po' Boy

SHRIMP

Peanut oil for deep-frying

12 large (size 16/20) shrimp, peeled and deveined

1 cup (140 g) finely ground cornmeal

½ cup (63 g) all-purpose flour

½ cup (50 g) Cajun Seasoning (page 22)

½ cup (118 ml) buttermilk

SANDWICH

2 hoagie rolls

¼ cup (63 g) Remoulade (page 130)

½ cup (28 g) shredded iceberg lettuce

2 plum tomatoes, cut ¼-inch (6 mm) thick

MAKES 2 SANDWICHES

In my dreams, I walk into a perfectly manicured backyard garden surrounded by my friends. The magnolias are in full bloom. Someone places a tall bourbon cocktail in my hand. I can smell the smoke and caramelizing meat of a well-tended barbecue pit and there—on the buffet table—next to a mountain of shucked oysters on ice, acres of deviled eggs, and a bowl of hush puppies, is a pile of shrimp po' boys stacked like cordwood. There's one for everybody, and they're still warm. I'm passing along this recipe because I want you to help make my dream come true.

INSTRUCTIONS

1. To make the shrimp, heat the peanut oil in a deep-fryer or Dutch oven to 350°F (177°C). Set out a wire rack for draining the fried shrimp.

2. Make a dredge for the shrimp by combining the cornmeal, all-purpose flour, and Cajun Seasoning in a bowl. Submerge the shrimp in the buttermilk. Remove them, let them dry briefly, then toss them to coat in the dredge.

3. Working in batches, fry the shrimp for 2 to 3 minutes until golden brown and cooked through. Drain briefly on the wire rack.

4. To assemble the sandwiches, slather the insides of the hoagie rolls generously with the remoulade.

5. Add the iceberg lettuce and sliced tomato, and finish with the breaded shrimp, fresh out of the deep-fryer. Serve immediately.

1 cup (225 g) heavy mayonnaise, preferably Duke's Real Mayonnaise

1 tablespoon (11 g) smooth Dijon mustard

1 teaspoon whole-grain Dijon mustard

1 tablespoon (4 g) chopped flat-leaf parsley

1 tablespoon (15 ml) habanero hot sauce, preferably Cry Baby Craig's Hot Sauce

1 tablespoon (15 ml) fresh lemon juice

1 teaspoon Worcestershire sauce

2 garlic cloves, minced

2 teaspoons capers, coarsely chopped

1 scallion, thinly sliced

1 teaspoon smoked paprika

**MAKES ABOUT
1½ CUPS (375 G)**

REMOULADE

Something happens to everything above your shoulders after your first experience with remoulade—whether you used it as a dipping sauce or slathered it on a hoagie bun as a foundation for your sandwich. Your mouth tends to relax a little, you smile more, you start slipping *au bon* this or *c'est bon* that into your conversation, and you develop an undeniable craving to grip a strong cocktail in a hurricane glass while swaying to the recorded works of Professor Longhair. While the condition comes and goes, it never really leaves you—and you're a better person for it.

INSTRUCTIONS ───────────────

1. Combine the mayonnaise, mustards, parsley, hot sauce, lemon juice, Worcestershire sauce, garlic, capers, scallion, and paprika in a medium bowl. Whisk together.

2. Use immediately or store in an airtight container in your refrigerator.

Tennessee Hot Chicken Sandwich

2 **boneless** Fried Buttermilk Chicken
(page 142)

2 **cups (360 g)** Tennessee Hot Sauce
(page 34)

¼ **cup (58 g)** Cry Baby Craig's Aîoli
(page 123)

2 **burger buns**, halved

½ **cup (28 g)** shredded iceberg lettuce

8 **chips** of Spicy Cucumber Pickles
(page 40)

MAKES 2 SANDWICHES

I make no secret of my love for drive-thru fast food—particularly fried chicken sandwiches. When I was in Atlanta for college, before kitchens had become my real calling, I was introduced to a few not-so-great versions of Tennessee hot chicken and wasn't much impressed. Years later, when I was first introduced to the high octane of Hattie B's Hot Chicken and Prince's Hot Chicken in Nashville, they were revelations. (I'm from Minnesota—how could they not be?) No one can do what they do, but together, with this recipe, we can get pretty damn close. Have that plate with a paper towel ready to go before you slip the double-dredged bird in the hot oil. Letting some of the fry drip off when it comes out crispy ensures that the sauce will evenly coat the breading.

INSTRUCTIONS ─────────────

1. Fry the chicken according to the recipe and allow to drain momentarily. Put the Tennessee Hot in a small saucepan over low heat to melt it. Dunk the cooked chicken into the hot sauce until fully coated, then allow to drain briefly on a paper towel–lined plate.

2. Spread the aîoli generously on both the tops and bottoms of the buns. Pile the lettuce and pickles on the bottom buns, then add the fried chicken and serve.

MAINS

7

Now we get to the meat of the matter—literally and figuratively. When planning a dinner party or, let's face it, just dinner, the first thing we tend to consider is the star of the show—and in my world, that usually takes the form of a delicious creature that once walked, flew, or swam. Since planning your menu is similar to selecting your playlist, remember that with all the considerations and allowances you'll make for your guests, you're still the DJ, and the vinyl is coming from your crate. Choose a main course that not only will get the oohs and aahs of your guests, but will also groove with you first. Start with the recipe you can put your passions into.

I not only want the recipes in this book to introduce you to ingredients and flavors you may have never seen before, but I also want them to inspire your imagination and your confidence, your desire to share the best parts of your heart with others through food. At the end of the day, that's really all it's about. When I was a young boy and I asked for an Easy-Bake Oven, it was only partly because I wanted to crush my own cupcakes at will without waiting for my mom or grandma to make them for me. The real reason was because I wanted to taste and provide the same kind of love they gave me when they cooked and baked for me and my brothers. Learning to understand that, cultivate it, and act on it laid the foundation of my Northern Soul.

The compositions of these main courses are pretty varied and their flavors are bold. While a few of them can stand on their own as a meal, most beg to be paired with the starters and sides, appetizers, soups, and salads you will find elsewhere in this book. Don't overthink it. Pick out what you like, what you're in the mood to eat, and make notes on what works and what doesn't. Go bold. Make some noise and bring everyone along for the ride.

Biscuits and Gravy

GRAVY

1 pound (455 g) ground pork

1 pound (455 g) bacon, finely chopped

1 medium yellow onion, diced

2½ teaspoons (8 g) minced garlic

2½ teaspoons (2 g) chopped
fresh thyme

1 tablespoon (2 g) chopped
fresh rosemary

¾ cup plus 1 tablespoon (102 g)
all-purpose flour

2 teaspoons kosher salt

1 tablespoon (6 g) freshly
ground black pepper

6½ cups (1.5 L) whole milk

7 tablespoons (98 g) unsalted butter

TO ASSEMBLE

4 eggs

8 Buttermilk Biscuits,
recipe page 80 or store-bought

¼ cup (80 g) chopped Pickled
Fresno Chiles, (page 44)

SERVES 4

I used to work for a guy who didn't abide by hangovers, his own or anyone else's. No matter how hard he and his staff rocked the "shifties" (after-shift shots, beers, or tumblers of wine), no matter how early that alarm for brunch service went off, his rule was "Big Boy/Girl Night = Big Boy/Girl Day." Life is always going to be about getting back on the horse and back to the grind—back to life, back to reality. Whether you queue up Hi-Tek or Soul II Soul, the message is the same: whatever you want, you've gotta work for it—and hard work requires calories. Biscuits and gravy are the OG field-hand fuel, especially when crowned with farm-fresh eggs. If you're not up and at 'em and out to conquer after a plate of biscuits and gravy, check your planner and slate a couple of hours for an early afternoon nap.

INSTRUCTIONS —————————

1. To make the gravy: In a large skillet, combine the ground pork, bacon, onion, and garlic. Cook over medium heat until the pork is browned and crumbles, 6 to 8 minutes. Add the thyme and rosemary and cook just until fragrant, about 30 seconds. Stir in the flour, salt, and pepper and cook for 1 minute, stirring constantly. Slowly pour in the milk, stirring constantly until the flour is mixed thoroughly with the liquid.

2. Bring the mixture to a simmer and stir often until the mixture thickens to a medium-thick gravy, about 5 to 7 minutes. Add the butter and stir until it is well incorporated. Taste, adjust the seasoning if you'd like, and keep warm over low heat.

3. To assemble the dish: Fry the eggs. Warm up the biscuits, split them in half using a fork, and divide the biscuit halves equally among four plates. Ladle the warmed gravy in equal portions over the biscuits, then place 1 egg on top of each biscuit. Garnish with pickled fresno chiles. This recipe makes a substantial amount of gravy; you can use it all for the 4 servings here, if you'd like, or you can use less and store the leftover gravy for 3 to 4 days in an airtight container in the refrigerator.

Smoked Brisket

One medium brisket, about 12-lb (5.4 kg)

¼ cups (340 g) Brisket Rub, page 24

2 tablespoons (30 ml) liquid smoke, if you are using an oven

Assorted barbecue sauces and pickles, for serving

SERVES 12 TO 16

A perfectly smoked brisket is the holy grail of BBQ. In competition barbecue there is a lot of talk of "bark," "smoke rings," and other desired features. Attempting this at home can seem daunting. Well, it doesn't have to be! Competition BBQ is something that even I don't do. In the words of my good friend and BBQ master Bryan Furman, "I don't cook for the judges, I cook for the people." In your case, the people are your friends and family—or, heck, maybe it's just for you and *you* are your people. Regardless, what's important with brisket is that it is tender and juicy and tastes delicious. Here are some tips on cooking the perfect brisket:

Select your brisket: There are many grades of beef from select up to top-end Wagyu. The higher the grade, the higher the price and the higher the quality. Choose what seems right for your occasion and your wallet. Then buy a half pound (225 g) more meat per person than you plan to serve. Between trimming and cooking the brisket, it will lose a fair amount of weight.

Trim your brisket: There are differing schools of thoughts on this. Some like to trim all the fat and some don't trim any. I fall somewhere in the middle; I like to take off large, thick chunks but I always leave a nice layer of fat. Fat equals flavor and moisture. For those trying to eat healthier, you can always cut off fat after the meat is served to you.

Rub and season your brisket: You can be a purist and go straight salt and pepper, which can yield amazing results—especially when using higher-quality grades of beef cooked in a powerful smoker. But I love flavor, and this is the perfect opportunity to use my signature Brisket Rub, on page 24.

1. Pull your brisket from the refrigerator and allow it to come to room temperature, so that the meat will loosen up, which allows for better absorption of seasonings. Generously rub the brisket with Brisket Rub, getting in every crevice; this is a very special time between you and your chosen brisket! Wash your hands first and do it bare-handed, becoming one with the brisket. Rub it down and let it rest in the refrigerator a minimum of 1 hour but up to 24 hours.

2. *If using a smoker or pellet grill:* Preheat to between 200 and 220°F (93 and 104°C). Insert a meat thermometer into the thickest part of the brisket and smoke to an internal temperature of 170 to 180°F (77 to 82°C), about 10 to 12 hours. Remove the brisket from the smoker and let it rest 30 minutes to 1 hour. Slice and enjoy with some Bourbon BBQ Sauce, page 20, or another barbecue sauce that you like, and pickles.

   If using an oven: Preheat the oven to 250°F (120°C). Place the brisket on a roasting rack in a roasting pan. Fill the bottom of the roasting pan with about 2 cups of water (475 ml) and the liquid smoke. Cover tightly with aluminum foil and cook to an internal temp of 140°F (60°C), then remove the foil and continue to cook to an internal temp of 180°F (82°C). These two stages can take anywhere from 5 to 8 hours. When the brisket is done, let it rest for 30 minutes to 1 hour. Slice and enjoy with Bourbon BBQ Sauce, page 20, or another barbecue sauce that you like, and pickles.

   Note: No matter how you choose to cook your brisket, just remember that the brisket is done when the brisket is done: There's nothing you can do to "cook it faster." Relax, have a drink, turn on some tunes, and let the time and temperature do the work.

Roasted Pork Shoulder

¼ cup (50 g) sugar

¼ cup (75 g) kosher salt

2 tablespoons (13 g) freshly ground black pepper, preferably coarse-ground

2 pounds (907 g) boneless pork shoulder

SERVES 4 TO 6

USE THIS IN THE CAROLINA BBQ SANDWICH ON PAGE 114.

Pork shoulder is a perfect exercise in the importance of rubs: with the right balance of time, temperature, sweetness, salt, and heat, the seams of fat in the pork shoulder become a superhighway of flavor, carrying the taste of the rub throughout the meat during the low and slow roasting process. Remember that for the best results, this is an overnight process, so clear out plenty of space in your fridge to let the rubbed pork roast cure overnight.

INSTRUCTIONS ─────────

1. Make a rub by combining the sugar, salt, and black pepper in a bowl. Using your hands, rub the mixture liberally onto the pork shoulder, including any nooks and crannies. Transfer to a plate or platter, cover loosely with plastic wrap, and allow to cure overnight in your refrigerator.

2. Preheat your oven to 450°F (230 °C). Transfer the pork shoulder to a roasting pan deep enough for the pork to be covered by water. Roast the pork uncovered for 20 minutes until the surface starts to get crispy and lightly charred. Remove from the oven and cover the pork with water to about 1 inch (2.5 cm) from the top, then cover tightly with foil. Return the roasting pan to the oven and turn the oven down to 275°F (140°C), then braise the meat for 2½ to 3 hours until it is fully cooked and tender.

3. Carefully remove the pork from the liquid and transfer to a heat-proof bowl. While it is still hot, use gloved hands to pull the pork into large bite-sized chunks without shredding the meat. Serve in sandwiches or on a plate alongside your favorite sides.

   Note: Save the braising liquid after the pork is done cooking. It makes a great pork stock for other recipes.

BBQ Ribs

1 cup (70 g) Rib Rub, page 30

2 pounds (907 g) St. Louis–style pork ribs

½ cup (120 ml) apple cider, optional

SERVES 6 TO 8

I love ribs! There's nothing better than tearing the meat off the bone of perfectly cooked ribs: it's carnal, it's visceral, shoot, it's even sensual. There are many types of ribs, but for me the best are St. Louis–style pork ribs or spareribs. They are generally fattier and have more meat.

When selecting your ribs, ask your butcher or grocer if they have been peeled, which means the membrane on the back side of the rack has been removed. If not, you'll want to do this yourself to ensure the most tender result. Peel a corner of the membrane up with a knife or your fingers, and then, using a kitchen towel for a better grip, slowly peel it away.

Do not forget to rub the ribs generously ahead of time, preferably at least 12 hours. If you like extra heat, add some more cayenne to the rub.

INSTRUCTIONS

1. Rub the spareribs liberally with the Rib Rub, making sure to rub the sides and cracks as well as the top and bottom surfaces. Let the ribs rest in the refrigerator for at least 1 hour but up to 24 hours.

2. *If using a grill or smoker:* Preheat it to 375°F (190°C). Place the ribs bone side down on the grate and cook, with the lid down, for 30 minutes. Remove the ribs and wrap them tightly in aluminum foil; if you like, do what I do and drizzle the ribs with some apple cider before you wrap them in foil. Return the ribs to the grill or smoker and cook for 30 minutes more. Lower the heat to 275°F (140°C), unwrap the ribs, and cook them another 30 minutes or so, until they reach an internal temperature of 155°F (68°C). Remove them from the grill or smoker, let rest for 10 to 15 minutes, then slice them and serve.

   If using an oven: If you don't have a grill or smoker or it's January in Minnesota, you can still make these ribs in the oven. Preheat the oven to 350°F (180°C). Line a sheet pan with foil and place the ribs bone side down. Cook the ribs for 30 minutes. Remove the ribs from the oven and wrap them tightly in foil, drizzling them with a few tablespoons (45 ml) of apple cider first, if you like. Increase the oven temperature to 400°F (200°C) and cook the ribs for 30 minutes more. Remove and unwrap the ribs and lower the oven temperature to 300°F (150°C). Cook the ribs for about 20 minutes more, until they reach an internal temperature of 155°F (68°C). Remove the ribs from the oven and let them rest for 10 to 15 minutes. Slice and enjoy.

TOO MUCH IS SOMETIMES JUST ENOUGH

While food waste is a legitimate, pervasive issue in our country, the last thing you want to do as a "hospitalitarian" is run out of food. It's always a good idea when entertaining company to make that one extra dish and have those extra couple of portions on hand. Trust me. These recipes will blow your loved ones away, and they'll want more. What to do with leftovers? Instead of loading up on plastic resealables at the grocery store, go down to your neighborhood restaurant—the one you love that does those great soups and uses biodegradable take-out containers—and ask how much they would charge you for a dozen with lids. Pay what they ask—and leave a tip. When dinner is over and your brother-in-law is still eyeing the hush puppies and the last four shrimp on the serving platter, offer him a serving spoon and one of the take-out containers and tell him to go to town.

Fried Buttermilk Chicken

CHICKEN BRINE

2 quarts (1.9 L) water

½ cup plus 2 tablespoons (188 g) kosher salt

⅓ cup (67 g) sugar

2 garlic cloves, smashed

1 orange, halved

1 lemon, halved

1 jalapeño, halved lengthwise

2 sprigs fresh thyme

1 bay leaf

1 teaspoon whole black peppercorns

1 teaspoon yellow mustard seeds

½ teaspoon red pepper flakes

3 large ice cubes

CHICKEN

6 boneless, skinless chicken thighs

Peanut oil for deep-frying

2 cups (250 g) Chicken Dredge (page 26)

2 cups (470 ml) buttermilk

SERVES 3 TO 4

While your know-it-all uncle may have insisted brining is a crucial step for the Thanksgiving bird, brining isn't just for turkey. Chicken benefits extremely well from a soak in liquid flavor. It keeps the meat juicy during the cooking process and imparts distinctive flavors like heat level and saltiness or sweetness that you can custom control to your preferences. The important thing to remember is that after bringing all the ingredients to a boil, the brine must be completely chilled before you get your bird in the bath.

INSTRUCTIONS

1. To make the brine, combine the water, salt, sugar, garlic, orange, lemon, jalapeño, thyme, bay leaf, black peppercorns, mustard seeds, and red pepper flakes in a large pot. Bring to a boil. Remove from the heat and stir in the ice. Allow to cool completely before straining, discarding the solids. Do not use brine until it is completely cooled.

2. Brine the chicken thighs for 48 hours in an airtight container or plastic bag in the refrigerator.

3. To prepare the chicken, begin by heating the peanut oil in your countertop deep-fryer or Dutch oven to 325°F (163°C). Set up for dredging nearby with one bowl holding the dredge and another bowl holding the buttermilk.

4. Remove the chicken from the brine, dip it in the dredge, shake off the excess, then dip in the buttermilk, then back into the dredge. Do this for all the chicken, setting each piece aside on a wire rack until you are ready to fry it.

5. Working in batches if necessary, fry the chicken in the hot oil 6 to 10 minutes, until the chicken reaches an internal temperature of 165°F (74°C). Serve, or use in another dish, such as Chicken and Waffles (page 154), Tennessee Hot Chicken Sandwich (page 131), or Crispy Chicken Sandwiches (page 116).

Andouille Sausage

5 pounds (2.3 kg) ground pork

2¾ tablespoons (52 g) kosher salt

1½ teaspoons (6 g) pink curing salt (it is best to measure this ingredient by weight)

3½ teaspoons (8 g) smoked paprika

4 teaspoons (4 g) dried oregano

2 teaspoons onion powder

2 teaspoons gumbo filé powder

2 teaspoons freshly ground black pepper

1½ teaspoons freshly grated nutmeg

1 teaspoon mustard powder

1 teaspoon ground cloves

1 teaspoon ground allspice

¾ teaspoon smoke powder or ⅛ teaspoon liquid smoke

1 cup (235 ml) unsalted pork stock

2 tablespoons (20 g) minced garlic

**MAKES ABOUT
18 6-INCH (15 CM)
SAUSAGE LINKS**

Andouille is one of the cornerstones of traditional, Cajun-style Louisiana cooking and this recipe is definitely a level up in your skill set. However, it's like many of the other exercises in this collection of delicious madness in that after trying it two or three times, you know how to do something very few others can. The end results will provide you with a versatile staple you can pile high on a buffet table, simmer in every soup or stew imaginable, freeze for future use, or swap with your foodie friends for everything from artisan honey to rare sneakers and bitcoin.

INSTRUCTIONS ——————————

1. Place all the meat grinder parts in a freezer for at least 1 hour to ensure everything is as cold as you can get it. Prepare your sausage casings (preferably hog casings) according to the package (or your butcher's) instructions—usually by rinsing and soaking for 15 to 20 minutes in cold water.

2. Mix together the pork, kosher salt, pink curing salt, paprika, oregano, onion powder, filé powder, black pepper, nutmeg, mustard powder, cloves, allspice, smoke powder, pork stock, and garlic in a mixing bowl.

3. Assemble your meat grinder with a medium/coarse grinding plate. Grind the seasoned mixture through twice to ensure it is fully mixed and evenly ground before switching to a sausage-stuffing attachment on your meat grinder. Tie off one end of the hog casing and load it onto the stuffing tube. Begin stuffing. Every 6 inches (15 cm) or so, twist the casing to separate the sausage links. Refrigerate the sausages until you're ready to hot smoke them.

4. Preheat your smoker to 225°F (107°C) and cook the sausages until the internal temperature reaches 160° (71°C), about 45 minutes. Serve, or save in the refrigerator and use in another recipe, such as Creole Jambalaya (page 148).

Gumbo My Way

4 tablespoons (56 g) unsalted butter

¼ cup (31 g) all-purpose flour

1 tablespoon (15 ml) vegetable oil

8 ounces (225 g) bulk andouille sausage, homemade (recipe, page 143) or store-bought

4 garlic cloves, minced

2 cups (320 g) diced white onion

1 cup (150 g) diced green pepper

1 cup (120 g) diced celery

2 cups (455 g) frozen okra

1 cup (242 g) canned crushed tomatoes

1 cup (235 ml) chicken stock

1 cup (235 ml) pork stock (see page 138), or, if you do not have it, 1 additional cup (235 ml) chicken stock

1 pound (455 g) cooked boneless, skinless chicken breast cut into a medium dice

1 tablespoon (6 g) freshly ground black pepper

2 tablespoons (24 g) Cajun Seasoning, recipe page 22

3 tablespoons (45 ml) Worcestershire sauce

¼ cup (59 ml) fresh lemon juice

2 tablespoons (30 g) habanero hot sauce, such as Cry Baby Craig's Hot Sauce

2 cups (390 g) uncooked white rice

½ tablespoon (3 g) gumbo filé powder

4 tablespoons (24 g) thinly sliced scallions

SERVES 4 TO 6

Everybody has their recipe, and this one is mine.

INSTRUCTIONS ───────────

1. Heat the butter in a pan over medium heat. Whisk in the flour slowly and cook, whisking constantly, until you have a brown roux, about 10 minutes. Set the pan aside.

2. In a large skillet or Dutch oven, heat the vegetable oil over medium heat. Add the andouille and brown it heavily, 8 to 10 minutes. Add the garlic, onion, green pepper, celery, and okra and cook, stirring often, until the onion is soft and translucent, about 5 minutes.

3. Add the crushed tomatoes, stocks, and cooked chicken and stir to combine well. Bring to a boil and stir in the black pepper, Cajun Seasoning, Worcestershire sauce, lemon juice, and hot sauce. Reduce to a low simmer and cook, stirring occasionally, for 30 minutes. Meanwhile, cook the rice according to the package directions, and keep it warm once it is fully cooked.

4. Whisk the reserved roux into the chicken-andouille mixture, taking care to break up any lumps. If the sauce seems too thick, stir in some additional chicken stock to thin it. Return to a boil to activate the roux and cook, stirring often, for 5 minutes. Turn off the heat and stir in the gumbo filé powder.

5. Ladle the gumbo into individual serving bowls, then place a generous serving of rice in the middle of each bowl. Garnish with the scallions and serve.

Braised Oxtail with Sweet Potato Gnocchi

1 tablespoon (19 g) kosher salt

1 tablespoon (6 g) freshly ground black pepper

¾ teaspoon ground allspice

5 pounds (2.3 kg) oxtails

1 tablespoon plus 1 teaspoon (20 ml) extra virgin olive oil

4 shallots, coarsely chopped

4 carrots, coarsely chopped

3 celery ribs, coarsely chopped

3 garlic cloves, whole

1½ cups (353 ml) red wine

½ cup (130 g) tomato paste

½ bunch flat-leaf parsley

2 sprigs fresh rosemary

2 bay leaves

Zest of 1 lemon

Enough unsalted chicken stock, preferably homemade, to cover the oxtails (about 2 quarts/1.9 L)

FOR THE GNOCCHI

Two 8- to 10-ounce (225 to 280 g) sweet potatoes

1 garlic clove, pressed

½ cup (40 g) shredded Parmesan cheese

2 teaspoons salt

2 teaspoons white pepper

1 teaspoon ground nutmeg

2 large eggs

2 cups (250 g) all-purpose flour, plus more for rolling

SERVES 6

Oxtail is another superb representation of how enslaved African people seized the opportunity to turn scraps into sustenance. Popular all over the Southern states and the Caribbean, this cut is typically inexpensive and readily available at your local butcher shop. The dry-rub and overnight cure is part of the tenderizing process and doesn't work well with a rushed process, so be sure to give yourself plenty of time with this recipe.

INSTRUCTIONS ────────────

1. Mix the salt, pepper, and allspice together. Rub the seasoning all over the oxtails, cover, and allow to dry brine overnight.

2. The next day, preheat the oven to 325°F (163°C).

3. Heat the oil in a large braising pan or Dutch oven over medium heat and, working in batches as necessary to prevent crowding the pan, sear the oxtails on all sides until a deep golden brown. Remove the oxtails from the pan and set aside. To the same pan, add the shallots, carrots, celery, and garlic, reduce the heat to medium low, and cook for 5 minutes, scraping the browned bits off the bottom of the pan as you go. Add the wine and tomato paste, deglazing the bottom of the pot.

4. Return the oxtails to the pan and add the parsley, rosemary, bay leaves, and lemon zest. Pour the chicken stock over until the tails are fully submerged in liquid. Cover tightly or wrap with foil and braise in the oven for 3 to 3½ hours, until the meat is tender.

NORTHERN SOUL

5. While the oxtails are braising, make the gnocchi: Prick the sweet potatoes with a fork several times and microwave them for 5 to 6 minutes (or, if you prefer, bake them at 350° F for 40 minutes). Set aside until cool enough to handle, then peel and rice or mash them. Mix them in a bowl with the garlic, cheese, salt, pepper, garlic, nutmeg, and eggs. Then add the flour a little bit at a time until a pliable dough is formed.

6. Bring a large pot of lightly salted water to a boil. While the water comes to a boil, form the gnocchi. On a floured table, roll the dough out in several long "snakes," then cut the "snakes" into 1-inch (2.5 cm) pieces. Drop the pieces into the boiling water and allow them to cook until they float. Remove the floating gnocchi with a slotted spoon, drain any excess water, and set aside until the oxtails are cooked.

7. Remove the oxtails from the oven, uncover, and allow to cool. When the meat is cool enough to handle, pull it off the bones. Strain the braising liquid, discarding the solids. Return the liquid to the pan, skim the fat from the top, and reduce by half over medium-high heat. Season to taste with salt and pepper.

8. Sear the gnocchi on all sides in some butter in a large sauté pan over medium-high heat. When they are golden brown, stir in the oxtail ragout, heat the mixture through, and serve.

Creole Jambalaya

3 cups (537 g) uncooked red rice,
such as Jefferson red rice
from Anson Mills

2 tablespoons (28 g) unsalted butter

1 pound (455 g) boneless,
skinless chicken thighs

1 pound (455 g) andouille sausage,
store-bought or homemade (page 143)

¾ cup (180 ml) water

6 cups (1.4 L) Jambalaya Sauce
(opposite)

1 pound (455 g) shrimp (16/20-size)
with heads removed, peeled
and deveined

SERVES 6 TO 8

Every culture on the planet seems to have a venerated one-pot meal with rice as the star ingredient. India has *biryani*, Spain touts *paella*, and there are as many *risottos* as there are towns in Italy with a population numbering more than seven people. Even Holland has *rijsttafel*, a holdover from their days monopolizing the spice trade routes that took them to Indonesia. On our shores we have jambalaya—a dish with origins as complicated and opinionated as your spouse's uncle. A hallmark of New Orleans cuisine, the Creole French and Spanish roots of jambalaya usually come up first in culinary conversations, but the influence of jollof rice from West Africa—particularly Ghana, Nigeria, and Senegal—is pretty undeniable.

INSTRUCTIONS ──────────

1. Cook the rice according to the package instructions.

2. Meanwhile, melt the butter in a Dutch oven or heavy skillet over medium heat. When the foaming subsides, add the chicken thighs and sear on each side, working in batches as necessary to avoid crowding the pan. Transfer the seared chicken to a plate; don't worry about the chicken being raw in the middle just yet—we're going to finish cooking it shortly.

3. Add the sausage to the pan and continue to cook, stirring occasionally, until the sausage is nicely browned, about 6 minutes. By this point there should be some nice dark brown bits (the fond) on the bottom of the pan. Pour in the water and use a wooden spoon to scrape up the browned bits. Return the chicken to the pot and add the Jambalaya Sauce. Stir to combine and bring to a simmer. Simmer, covered, for 30 to 40 minutes, until the chicken is fully cooked and fork tender, but not yet falling apart.

4. Stir in the shrimp and cook, uncovered, for 4 to 5 minutes, until the shrimp is fully cooked.

5. Serve in a bowl with the rice on the bottom and the chicken, sausage, shrimp, and Jambalaya Sauce ladled equally over the top.

Jambalaya Sauce

1 28-ounce can (794 g) plum tomatoes in liquid

2 tablespoons (30 ml) Worcestershire sauce

1 tablespoon (15 ml) habanero hot sauce, such as Cry Baby Craig's

2 cups (475 ml) fish stock or chicken stock

2 tablespoons (14 g) Cajun Seasoning, page 22

2 teaspoons smoked paprika

2 tablespoons (14 g) Old Bay seasoning

1 teaspoon celery seed

3 tablespoons (40 g) bacon fat

1 medium yellow onion, julienned

2 celery ribs, cut into ¼-inch (6 mm) slices

1 green bell pepper, julienned

1 jalapeno pepper, seeded and julienned

2 garlic cloves, minced

MAKES ABOUT 6 CUPS

Here's the source of the unmistakable and irresistible heat that powers this one-pot wonder. Relax, it's going to work with all of your favorite protein combos.

INSTRUCTIONS ────────────

1. Combine the canned tomatoes, Worcestershire, hot sauce, stock, Cajun Seasoning, smoked paprika, Old Bay, and celery seed and blend well with an immersion blender. Or you can add the ingredients to the jar of a conventional blender and blend well.

2. Heat the bacon fat in a skillet over medium heat. Add the onion, celery, bell pepper, jalapeno, and garlic and cook, stirring occasionally, until the onions are translucent and the vegetables are soft but not caramelized, about 10 minutes.

3. Pour the blended tomato mixture into the skillet and simmer, stirring occasionally, until the liquid is reduced by one third, about 10 minutes more.

Lobster Etouffee

6 **tablespoons (85 g)** unsalted butter

2 **cups (320 g)** diced white onion

1 **cup (150 g)** diced green pepper

1 **cup (120 g)** diced celery

4 **garlic cloves**, minced

¼ **cup (31 g)** all-purpose flour

2 **cups (390 g)** uncooked white rice

2 **quarts (1.9 L)** shellfish stock, seafood stock, or fish stock

1 **(15.5 ounce / 439 g) can** whole tomatoes, drained and coarsely chopped

3 **tablespoons (36 g)** Cajun Seasoning, recipe page 22

1 **tablespoon (15 g)** habanero hot sauce, such as Cry Baby Craig's Hot Sauce

1 **tablespoon (2 g)** fresh thyme leaves

2 **bay leaves**

2 **tablespoons (28 ml)** Worcestershire sauce

¼ **cup (59 ml)** fresh lemon juice

8 **ounces (225 g)** frozen and thawed lobster claw meat

Salt and freshly ground black pepper to taste

4 **small to medium lobster tails**

4 **lemon wedges**

SERVES 4

*E*touffee means stuffed or smothered. This dish is smothered in deliciousness, not to mention topped with a whole lobster tail. This ain't your grandmas etouffee.

INSTRUCTIONS ———————————

1. In a large skillet or Dutch oven, melt 4 tablespoons (55 g) of the butter over medium heat. Add the onion, green pepper, celery, and garlic and cook for 2 minutes, stirring often. Whisk in the flour until a roux just begins to form, 2 to 3 minutes more.

2. Cook the rice according to the package instructions and keep warm, if necessary, until it is needed.

3. Add the stock to the vegetable-roux mixture and stir thoroughly, taking care that there are no lumps in the roux. Add the tomatoes, 2 tablespoons (24 g) of the Cajun Seasoning, hot sauce, thyme, bay leaves, Worcestershire sauce, and lemon juice. Bring to a low simmer and cook for 30 minutes, stirring occasionally.

4. Add the lobster meat and cook for 5 minutes more. Add some additional stock if the sauce is too thick. Add salt and pepper to taste and keep the mixture warm over low heat.

5. With kitchen scissors, cut a slit in the top of each lobster tail from the front to the end of the tail. Using a fork or spoon, pull the tail meat out through the slit and let it rest on top of the shell.

6. Preheat the broiler to 500°F (250°C). Meanwhile, transfer the tails to a broiler-ready sheet pan. In a separate pan, melt the remaining 2 tablespoons (28 g) of butter. Brush this butter onto the lobster tail meat and sprinkle the remaining 1 tablespoon (12 g) of Cajun Seasoning on top. Broil the tails for 6 to 8 minutes, until the meat is cooked through.

7. Divide the rice among 4 plates. Pour the sauce over the rice and top each serving with a lobster tail. Serve with lemon wedges.

Chicken Stew with Ramp-Ricotta Dumplings

STOCK

1 3- to 4-pound (1.4 to 1.8 kg)
stewer chicken

1 medium yellow onion, roughly chopped

6 garlic cloves, smashed

4 celery ribs, roughly chopped

2 carrots, roughly chopped

4 tablespoons (20 g) whole
black peppercorns

2 sprigs fresh tarragon

4 sprigs fresh thyme

8 bay leaves

STEW

1 cup (225 g) unsalted butter

1 cup (125 g) all-purpose flour

2 cups (320 g) diced yellow onion

½ cup (45 g) diced fennel bulb

4 celery ribs, diced

2 carrots, diced

2 garlic cloves, minced

½ cup (30 g) chopped flat-leaf parsley

2 tablespoons (5 g) chopped
fresh thyme leaves

2 tablespoons (8 g) chopped
fresh tarragon leaves

1 tablespoon (3.6 g) red pepper flakes

2 tablespoons (18 g) garlic powder

2 tablespoons (14 g) onion powder

6 tablespoons (90 ml) dry vermouth

2 tablespoons (30 ml) champagne vinegar

Salt and freshly ground pepper to taste

One recipe (24 dumplings)
Ramp-Ricotta Dumplings
(see opposite)

SERVES 8 TO 10

This is one of my favorite seasonal comfort food dishes and a great introduction to several necessary exercises of technique: making stock, making dumplings, and making stew. Mastering those three will provide you with the skills to successfully feed anyone, anywhere on planet Earth.

INSTRUCTIONS

1. To make the stock: Add the chicken, onion, garlic, celery, carrots, black peppercorns, tarragon, thyme, and bay leaves to a large stockpot. Add enough cold water to cover the chicken by 1 inch (2.5 cm). Bring to a boil, then reduce to a simmer and cook, covered, until the chicken is falling off the bone, about 1¾ hours.

2. Carefully remove the chicken from the stock and, once it is cool enough to handle, shred the chicken meat, discarding the skin and bones. Strain the stock, discarding the solids and keeping the liquid.

3. To make the stew: Melt the butter over medium-low heat in a stockpot or Dutch oven. When the foaming subsides, whisk in the flour and cook, stirring constantly, until a blonde roux has been achieved, about 3 minutes. Add the onion, fennel, celery, carrots, and garlic and cook, stirring occasionally, until the vegetables are slightly softened but not at all browned, about 6 minutes.

4. Add the parsley, thyme, tarragon, red pepper flakes, and garlic and onion powders, cooking briefly until perfumey, about 30 seconds. Add the shredded chicken, vermouth, and vinegar, then whisk in your strained stock until the stew reaches your desired consistency. Bring to a simmer and cook for 10 minutes, seasoning to taste with salt and pepper.

5. Add the uncooked dumplings to the stew and cook them, stirring occasionally, until all the dumplings have puffed up and float, about 8 to 10 minutes. The dumplings should have a springy consistency. Ladle the stew and dumplings into individual serving bowls.

NORTHERN SOUL

1½ cups (134 g) ramp greens

2 pounds (910 g) ricotta cheese

2 large eggs

1 cup (100 g) grated
Pecorino Romano cheese

1½ cups (188 g) all-purpose flour,
plus more for dusting

4 teaspoons (25 g) kosher salt

2 tablespoons (12 g) freshly
ground black pepper

½ teaspoon freshly grated nutmeg

½ teaspoon cayenne pepper

MAKES 24 DUMPLINGS

RAMP-RICOTTA DUMPLINGS

Ramps, also called wild leeks, are a member of the allium family that grow wild all over rural stretches of North America east of the Mississippi River during springtime. They have a strong reputation as a forager's delight. If you can't get out and scrounge trails and shady pastures for them yourself, you can often find them at farmer's markets and food co-ops. You'll likely smell them before you see them; they have a robust, sweet, and pungent garlicky aroma. Few foods carry the flavor of Mother Nature coming to life after a long, cold winter more than do ramps on your dinner plate.

INSTRUCTIONS

1. Bring a small pot of water to a boil. Make an ice bath in a separate pot. Drop the fresh ramps into the boiling water and cook until wilted, 10 to 15 seconds. Remove immediately from the boiling water and transfer to the ice bath to chill quickly. When the ramps are cold, pull them out of the ice bath and squeeze to remove any excess liquid. Mince the blanched leaves.

2. Drain the ricotta.

3. In the bowl of a stand mixer fitted with the paddle attachment, combine the eggs, Pecorino, flour, salt, pepper, nutmeg, and cayenne. Mix until just combined, scraping down the sides as needed. Alternatively, mix with a hand-held electric mixer in a mixing bowl. Fold in the ricotta and ramps.

4. By hand, form the dumplings into discs about 1 inch (2.5 cm) in diameter and ½ inch (1 cm) thick. If you are making the dumplings ahead of time, you may dust the dumplings with flour and store them in an airtight container in the refrigerator. If you are using them right away, drop the dumplings into simmering liquid (such as the chicken stew in the recipe opposite) and cook until the dumplings have puffed up and float to the surface, about 10 minutes. To test if one is done, slice it in half and make sure the center is no longer raw and has a cooked and pillowy appearance.

Chicken and Waffles

WAFFLES

6 eggs, separated

6 cups (750 g) all-purpose flour

1½ tablespoons (19 g) sugar

¼ cup (110 g) baking powder

2 teaspoons (11 g) salt

3 cups (705 ml) whole milk

2¼ cups (530 ml) buttermilk

¾ cup (180 ml) vegetable oil

¾ cup (180 ml) extra virgin olive oil

1½ teaspoons (23 ml)
pure vanilla extract

CHICKEN

6 Fried Chicken Thighs (page 142)

3 cups (705 ml) Tennessee
Hot Sauce (page 34) (optional)

6 WAFFLES

6 tablespoons (83 g) Honey
Cayenne Butter (page 84)

1 cup (235 ml) bourbon
barrel–aged maple syrup, preferably,
or other maple syrup

2 cups (488 g) Pickled Pears (page 51)

SERVES 6

There are as many origin stories involved with chicken and waffles as there are seasons of *SNL* with Kenan Thompson as a cast member. At the end of the day, what really matters it that the waffles aren't too sweet, the chicken is juicy, and both are warm and crunchy. This rendition, with Tennessee hot seasoning and honey butter, will wake up anyone for breakfast, lunch, or dinner.

INSTRUCTIONS ————————

1. To make the waffles, beat the egg whites in the bowl of a stand mixer fitted with the whip attachment on medium-high speed until the whites form stiff peaks. (Alternatively, beat in a mixing bowl using a hand-held electric mixer.)

2. In a large bowl, whisk the egg yolks by hand until foamy and slightly pale. Add the flour, sugar, baking powder, salt, milk, buttermilk, vegetable and olive oils, and vanilla to the bowl with the yolks. Whisk together until just smooth, then fold in the egg whites. Set aside in the refrigerator while you prepare the chicken.

3. Fry the chicken, following the recipe provided. If you like it spicy, melt the Tennessee Hot Sauce in a small saucepan over low heat. When the chicken is done frying, dunk it in the sauce to submerge it thoroughly, then allow the chicken to drain briefly on a paper towel–lined plate.

4. Preheat your waffle iron. Once hot, grease liberally with nonstick spray, then ladle in the waffle batter and cook until crispy on the outside, fluffy on the inside, and golden brown in color.

5. To serve, smear each waffle with a generous dollop of honey butter, then top with the fried chicken. Drizzle the whole thing with maple syrup and serve with pickled pears alongside.

Braised Pork Cheek

4 pounds (1.8 kg) pork cheeks

2 tablespoons (38 g) kosher salt

8 teaspoons (48 g) freshly
ground black pepper

4 tablespoons (52 g) bacon fat

2 tablespoons (20 g) minced garlic

1½ cups (240 g) chopped yellow onion

1 cup (130 g) chopped carrot

2 cups (360 g) chopped plum tomatoes

4 sprigs fresh rosemary

2 teaspoons red pepper flakes

3 quarts (2.8 L) chicken stock

4 bay leaves

3¼ cups and ¼ cup
(823 ml) bourbon

2 tablespoons (30 g) light brown sugar

SERVES 6 TO 8

Pork cheeks won't typically be found next to the tenderloins and roasts at the grocery store. This recipe will probably require a phone call to your local butcher shop and perhaps even a pre-order. The effort is well worth it as the end result is a luscious and tender preparation unlike any other cut of meat.

INSTRUCTIONS ——————————

1. Trim the cheeks of excess fat and gristle and season with salt and pepper. Heat the bacon fat in a large braising pan or Dutch oven over medium heat. Working in batches to prevent crowding in the pan, sear the pork cheeks until each side is a deep golden brown, about 6 minutes per side. When the cheeks are seared, remove to a paper towel–lined plate.

2. Add the garlic, onion, and carrot to the pan and reduce the heat to medium-low. Cook, scraping the browned bits off the bottom as you go, until the onions are translucent, roughly 8 minutes. Turn off the heat, then add the tomatoes, rosemary, red pepper flakes, chicken stock, bay leaves, and 3¼ cups (763 ml) of the bourbon (reserving the remaining ¼ cup [60 ml] for later).

3. Add the pork cheeks back to the pan, bring to a simmer, then cover with a tight-fitting lid. Cook, covered, until the cheeks are tender but not falling apart, about 50 minutes. Carefully remove the pork cheeks from the braising liquid and set aside and keep warm until ready to serve.

4. Strain the liquid, discarding the solids and returning the liquid to the pan. Skim the fat from the top, then bring the liquid to a boil and reduce it until you have a sauce that has thickened enough to coat the back of a spoon. Stir in the reserved ¼ cup (60 ml) of bourbon and the brown sugar.

5. Serve the pork cheeks on a bed of Braised Chard (page 78) or Black-Eyed Peas (page 76) with the sauce you made from the reduced braising liquid drizzled over the top.

NORTHERN SOUL

WINTER IS CELEBRATED HERE IN THE BOLD NORTH

The land of 10,000 lakes really has thousands more . . . and they all freeze in the winter. Get outside and enjoy yourself!

Bourbon Mussels

4 **bacon slices**, chopped

8 ounces (225 g) andouille sausage, homemade (recipe, page 143) or store-bought

4 Fresno chiles

4 garlic cloves, minced

2 medium shallots, coarsely chopped

8 ounces (235 ml) bourbon

2 (15.5 ounce / 439 g) cans whole tomatoes, drained and coarsely chopped

1½ teaspoons crushed red pepper

1 teaspoon liquid smoke

3 pounds (1.36 kg) fresh mussels in their shells, such as PEI mussels or your favorite variety

9 ounces (253 g) butter

Salt and freshly ground black pepper to taste

1 bunch flat-leaf parsley, chopped

4–6 lemon wedges

SERVES 4 TO 6

How do you make mussels come out of their shell? You get 'em drunk! Be sure to have some crusty bread close by so you can sop up all this bourbon-laced sauce.

INSTRUCTIONS ——————

1. Cook the bacon in a large skillet or Dutch oven over medium heat until it renders its fat and is brown and crisp, about 6 minutes. Add the andouille and cook about 6 minutes more, until the sausage is nicely browned.

2. Add the Fresno chiles, garlic, and shallots and cook for 2 minutes more, until the vegetables start to soften. Add the bourbon and use it to deglaze the pan for 2 to 3 minutes, until the alcohol has burned off. Add the tomatoes, crushed red pepper, and liquid smoke, bring to a boil, then immediately reduce to a simmer.

3. Add the mussels, cover the pan, and steam for 5 to 7 minutes, until the shells open. Once they have opened, add the butter to the sauce and stir to incorporate it. Add salt and pepper to taste. Garnish each serving with parsley and serve with a fresh lemon wedge.

Pimiento Cheese Shrimp and Grits

GRITS

2 cups (275 g) coarse-ground corn grits

4 cups (940 ml) water

4 cups (940 ml) whole milk

¼ cup (60 g) cream cheese at room temperature

¼ cup (30 g) shredded cheddar cheese

2 tablespoons (30 g) sour cream

¼ cup (45 g) diced pimiento peppers

4 tablespoons (56 g) unsalted butter

Kosher salt and freshly ground black pepper

SHRIMP

2 tablespoons (30 ml) vegetable oil

2 cups (300 g) julienned country ham (prosciutto, bacon, or any cured ham product will work)

4 tablespoons (56 g) unsalted butter

¼ cup (38 g) finely diced green bell pepper

¼ cup (20 g) finely diced yellow onion

¼ cup (30 g) finely diced celery

2 teaspoons minced garlic cloves

2 tablespoons (16 g) all-purpose flour

2 cups (470 ml) homemade unsalted shellfish stock or homemade or store-bought unsalted vegetable stock

¼ cup (45 g) diced canned tomatoes

1 tablespoon (7 g) Old Bay Seasoning

2 teaspoons Cajun Seasoning (page 22)

1 teaspoon cayenne pepper

1 teaspoon celery seeds

½ pound (228 g) shrimp (16/20-size), peeled and deveined

Juice of ½ lemon

2 tablespoons (12 g) sliced scallions

SERVES 4 TO 6

I can't really think of many meals that cover all of the bases the way that this one does: the hearty comfort of a well-cooked pot of grits kicked up with the soul-nourishing creaminess of pimiento cheese; the sweet, clean texture of shrimp simmered in tomatoes with ham; and the layered, lingering heat of Old Bay and cayenne. To me, nothing tastes more like the sunshine and freedom of a summer day boating on the river than these flavors found in this dish. Because the grits take a while to cook, make the shrimp (starting with step 3) while the grits are cooking.

INSTRUCTIONS

1. To make the grits, combine the grits and water in a saucepan and bring to a low boil over medium heat. Reduce the heat to a simmer and cook, covered, until the water is almost entirely absorbed, about 15 minutes. Add the milk and cook, stirring frequently, until the grits are creamy and the milk has been fully absorbed, about 30 minutes.

2. Fold in the cream cheese, cheddar, and sour cream until fully incorporated. Then fold in the pimientos and butter. Season to taste with salt and pepper.

3. To make the shrimp, heat the vegetable oil in a large skillet over medium heat. When the oil shimmers, add the ham and cook until it is just starting to brown, about 6 minutes. Add 1 tablespoon (14 g) of the butter and continue to cook until the ham has fully browned and becomes crisp, 4 minutes more. Using a slotted spoon, transfer the ham to a paper towel–lined plate to drain.

4. Add another 2 tablespoons (28 g) of the butter to the skillet along with the green pepper, onion, celery, and garlic. Sauté until the vegetables start to soften, but not long enough for the vegetables to gain any color, about 6 minutes. Stir in the flour, cooking long enough to make a blonde roux, about 5 minutes.

5. Stir in the stock, tomatoes, Old Bay, Cajun Seasoning, cayenne, and celery seeds. Bring to a simmer, add the shrimp, and cook for 4 minutes until the shrimp are plump, pink, and fully cooked. Then season with the lemon juice and salt and pepper to taste. Turn off the heat and stir in the remaining 1 tablespoon (14 g) butter.

6. Serve the grits in a bowl, topped with the shrimp and sauce, and garnished with the crisped country ham and sliced scallions.

Catfish and Grits
with Braised Chard and Tasso Vinaigrette

1 recipe Braised Chard (page 78), kept warm

FOR THE TASSO VINAIGRETTE

¼ cup (40 g) minced shallot

½ teaspoon kosher salt

½ cup (75 g) finely diced tasso ham

2 garlic cloves, minced

4 tablespoons (16 g) stemmed and chopped fresh oregano

4 tablespoons (10 g) stemmed and chopped fresh thyme

4 tablespoons (16 g) stemmed and chopped flat-leaf parsley

¾ teaspoon smoked paprika

½ teaspoon Aleppo chili pepper

1 tablespoon (6 g) lemon zest

1 cup (235 ml) red wine vinegar

½ cup (120 ml) extra virgin olive oil

FOR THE GRITS

2 cups (460 g) coarse-ground grits

4 cups (940 ml) water

4 cups (940 ml) whole milk

¼ cup (60 g) cream cheese at room temperature

½ cup (65 g) chopped roasted garlic (see Note)

3 tablespoons (6 g) coarse-ground black pepper

6 tablespoons (85 g) unsalted butter

Kosher salt to taste

FOR THE CATFISH

1 cup (140 g) finely ground cornmeal

1 cup (120 g) all-purpose flour

¼ cup (30 g) Cajun Seasoning (page 22)

Four 6- to 8-ounce (170 to 225 g) catfish fillets

Vegetable oil, for sautéing

Salt and black pepper to taste

SERVES 4

Although fish and grits is undeniably a Southern staple, it originated in Native American dishes such as trout or walleye prepared with Indian corn or hominy. Catfish is a West African staple that eventually became a mainstay in the Southern fish fry. I think this version, topped with tasso vinaigrette, takes this timeless combination to the next level.

INSTRUCTIONS ────────

1. *Make the vinaigrette:* Toss the shallot and salt together and let sit for 30 minutes. Add the shallot and salt and all of the remaining ingredients except the olive oil to a mixing bowl and stir to combine. Slowly drizzle in the olive oil while whisking to emulsify. Taste to check for seasoning. Set aside while you prepare the grits and fish.

2. *Make the grits:* Combine the grits and water in a saucepan and bring to a low boil over medium heat. Reduce the heat to very low and cook, covered, until all the water is almost entirely absorbed by the grits, about 15 minutes. Add the milk and cook, stirring frequently, until the grits are creamy and the milk is fully absorbed, about 30 minutes. Fold in the cream cheese until it is fully absorbed, then fold in the remaining ingredients.

3. *Make the fish:* Combine the cornmeal, flour, and Cajun Seasoning in a shallow bowl. Dredge the catfish fillets in this mixture to coat them on both sides. Heat about 1 inch (2.5 cm) of vegetable oil over medium-high heat in a large sauté pan. Once hot, cook the catfish fillets for 4 minutes on each side until cooked through and golden brown. Remove with a spatula or slotted spoon and place on paper towels to drain. Season the fillets with salt and pepper.

4. To serve, spoon a generous layer of grits onto each person's plate. Top with a layer of the Braised Chard. Top each serving with a catfish fillet, then drizzle some vinaigrette over each serving.

Note: To roast garlic, coat the garlic cloves with olive oil, place them in a baking dish or pan, and cook them, covered with aluminum foil, for 30 to 35 minutes in a 350°F (180°C) oven.

Low Country Seafood Boil

8 quarts (7.6 L) Seafood Boil Broth (page 164)

3 pounds (1.4 kg) new potatoes, quartered

1 pound (455 g) whole crawfish, purged (see note below)

1 pound (455 g) mussels, purged and beard removed

1 pound (455 g) whole 10/12-size shrimp, rinsed

5 ears of corn, shucked and halved

1 pound (455 g) andouille sausage, store-bought or homemade (page 143)

1½ cups (353 ml) Seafood Boil Butter (page 165)

SERVES 12 TO 14

Announce the arrival of this one on the banquet table by cranking up the volume on Christina Aguilera's breakout hit "Dirrty," because that's how things are about to get for you and your people. The key to finishing this one properly is quick timing for removing the ingredients from the broth and tossing them in the Seafood Boil Butter. Rather than dumping the lot into a colander and sending the boil down the drain of your overloaded sink, I recommend you take a trip to the nearest Asian grocery store and add what's called a "spider strainer" to your kitchen tool kit. It has a long bamboo handle with what looks like a round, concave, stainless steel spiderweb on the end. If you grew up in my part of the world, you'd imagine using it to clear out the hole you drilled in the lake for ice fishing. Place your large stainless steel mixing bowl next to the pot of boil and the pot of butter, then use the spider strainer to fish the ingredients out of the pot before you drop them in the bowl and give them a butter bath. I've recommended a couple of later uses for the broth, but in the meantime, make the music loud, pile the napkins high and shake your hips like Christina while you carry this party to the table.

INSTRUCTIONS ————————

1. In a large stockpot, bring the seafood boil broth to a rolling boil over high heat.

2. Add the potatoes to the boiling broth, and cook for 7 minutes, until the potatoes are just barely tender. Add the crawfish and continue cooking for 4 minutes. Add the mussels and shrimp, and continue cooking for 4 minutes. Add the corn and sausage and cook for 5 minutes.

3. At this point the crawfish should be bright red, the mussels open, the shrimp pink and fully cooked, the corn plump and bright yellow, and the potatoes tender. Remove the seafood and potatoes with a spider strainer, toss everything with the Seafood Boil Butter to season and serve immediately.

Note: Everything should be cooked in the same pot. Different ingredients will take different amounts of time to cook, so stagger adding ingredients to the pot as noted to ensure everything is done cooking at the same time. Feel free to experiment with different types of seafood, too. Lobster, crab, or clams are great additions or substitutes.

Tops from **2 fennel bulbs**, chopped

12 sprigs fresh thyme

4 sprigs fresh rosemary

6 tablespoons (113 g) whole black peppercorns

4 bay leaves

2 tablespoons (11 g) dried oregano

8 quarts (7.6 L) water

3 bulbs garlic, cloves peeled and smashed

2 fennel bulbs

3 medium yellow onions, coarsely chopped

6 tablespoons (84 g) Zatarain's crab boil seasoning

½ cup plus 1 tablespoon (133 ml) habanero hot sauce, preferably Cry Baby Craig's Hot Sauce

5 lemons, halved and juiced

3 tablespoons (48 ml) Worcestershire sauce

6 celery ribs, coarsely chopped

2 Fresno chiles, stemmed and halved lengthwise

2 jalapeños, stemmed and halved lengthwise

**MAKES ABOUT
8 QUARTS (7.6 L)**

SEAFOOD BOIL BROTH

In addition to being the cornerstone of the seafood boil experience, this broth freezes well after straining and can be used as a base for soups, and pasta sauces, and for cooking rice as a pilaf.

INSTRUCTIONS ───────────

1. Make a sachet by wrapping the fennel tops, thyme, rosemary, peppercorns, bay leaves, and dried oregano into a cheesecloth square and tying it with butcher's twine.

2. Combine the sachet with the water, garlic, fennel bulbs, onions, crab boil seasoning, hot sauce, lemons and their juice, Worcestershire sauce, celery, Fresno chiles, and jalapeño in a large stockpot. Bring to a simmer and simmer for 2 hours. Discard the sachet. Using an immersion blender (or working in batches with a conventional blender), puree the remainder as much as possible, then pass through a fine-mesh chinois or strainer.

4 scallions, whites and greens separated

1 shallot, halved lengthwise

1 Fresno chile, stemmed

1 jalapeño, stemmed

6 garlic cloves, minced,
plus **6 whole garlic cloves**

**2 tablespoons plus 1 teaspoon
(44 g)** kosher salt

**1 tablespoon plus 2 teaspoons
(10 g)** freshly ground black pepper

1 pound (455 g) clarified butter or ghee

¼ cup (29 g) Cajun Seasoning
(page 22)

**MAKES ABOUT
2½ (588 ML) CUPS**

SEAFOOD BOIL BUTTER

Reading the recipe for this one makes it sound like a lot of effort, but it's really little more than putting a few vegetables on high heat until they're done, combining them in a blender with a few raw ingredients, and then adding the lot to some melted, clarified butter. After a few minutes in that bath, you've got Low Country liquid gold, baby.

INSTRUCTIONS ─────────────

1. Prepare a wood fire in a grill (preferably) or preheat the broiler. Spread the scallion bottoms (whites), shallot, Fresno and jalapeño chiles, and whole garlic on a grill grate over a wood flame or arrange on a baking sheet put under the broiler. Roast, turning occasionally, until everything has a nice rich char but is not burned. Allow to cool briefly.

2. Place the roasted items in a blender or food processor with the minced garlic, salt, and pepper and process until as smooth as possible.

3. Thinly slice the scallion tops (greens).

4. Warm the clarified butter in a small saucepan over low heat until just melted. Transfer the butter to a mixing bowl and add the roasted vegetable mixture, scallion tops, and Cajun Seasoning. Stir until fully incorporated.

COCKTAILS

I spend more time sitting at bars than standing behind them. So it's important for me to give credit where credit is due. Spencer Short was an instrumental part of our cocktail team at the original Handsome Hog location and over the years he has seen it all. With little more guidance from me than my oft-repeated mantra "whiskey forward," and my oft-expressed desire that Handsome Hog be a place of "approachable hospitality," he has been a big creative force for these drinks. Spencer conveys the vibe by teaching our staff how to tell the stories behind them as part of our approach to service. He established our batching program to ensure that our cocktails are executed deliciously and consistently.

Moreover, Spencer, as the kind of barkeep who loves to set you up with the magic combination of a beer and a shot, has exemplified our philosophy of unpretentious, accessible hospitality. By training and by example, he has led our team to understand that when we open up and spend the time to get to know our guests, the end result of their special requests can be legendary (see #dope, page 176).

At the end of the day, isn't that what being a good host is all about? Nothing about taking good care of the people you invite to share a meal with you or sit down to savor what we like to call Liquid Finery needs to be complicated. Nor do the ingredients you purchase. Just give gratitude and attention to your good company. Listen and provide. Sip slowly. Savor. Repeat.

We Smoke Anything

1¼ ounces (35 ml) George Dickel Rye or other fine rye

1 ounce (28 ml) Ansac Cognac or other fine cognac

¾ ounce (21 ml) sweet vermouth, such as Carpano Antica Formula

¼ ounce (7 ml) Tobacco-Infused Bénédictine (page 186)

2 dashes bitters, such as Peychaud's Aromatic Cocktail Bitters

1 large ice cube

Lemon twist, to garnish

MAKES 1 COCKTAIL

This is Spencer's love letter to Handsome Hog—the first restaurant I opened in Saint Paul, Minnesota—and the spirit of Northern Soul in liquid form. We Smoke Anything (essentially the mission statement of Handsome Hog) was initially conceived as our take on a famous New Orleans cocktail standard, the Vieux Carré. Mixed with different proportions than the original classic, this is a standard cigar-smoking cocktail with a touch of sweet but aromatic, smooth, and punchy. The many degrees of fun to be had with this cocktail begin within its preparation. Get a small bag of cherry wood smoker chips and a hand-held butane torch from your local hardware store. Drop a few scant ounces of the chips in a cast-iron pan, lightly torch the wood, and hold the glass over the chips to capture the smoke that rises from the embers in the pan. The glass will gather and hold the sweet campfire aroma in a little cloud. In addition to accentuating the layered flavors of the cocktail, it's a nice little piece of theater for your thirsty audience. Serve with a bow and a flourish.

INSTRUCTIONS ————————

1. To smoke the glass, line a very small cast-iron pan with cherry wood chips, torch the wood, and place the glass on the small fire upside down until it extinguishes the fire and the smoke fills the glass.

2. Combine the rye, cognac, sweet vermouth, infused Bénédictine, and bitters in a mixing glass. Stir gently until the ice begins to melt, 15 to 20 revolutions. Pour the drink over a whiskey rock in a large rocks glass. Serve with a lemon twist.

    Note: To scale up for four people, use 5 ounces (140 ml) rye, 4 ounces (112 ml) cognac, 3 ounces (84 ml) sweet vermouth, 1 ounce (28 ml) of the infused Bénédictine, and ½ ounce (14 ml) bitters.

I Drink and I Know Things

1½ ounces (42 ml) Four Roses Bourbon
or other fine bourbon

¾ ounce (21 ml) Bénédictine D.O.M.

½ ounce (14 ml) allspice dram,
such as St. Elizabeth Allspice Dram

3 dashes Bolivar bitters,
such as Bittercube Bolivar Bitters*

1 large ice cube

1 sprig rosemary, to garnish

MAKES 1 COCKTAIL

Handsome Hog has a long and storied—and, to some, obnoxious—tradition of exercising the opposite of brevity when it comes to naming our cocktails. Spencer often remarks that it takes him an afternoon to write a cocktail menu and three weeks to give the drinks their names. Our former special events guru, Jane-of-all-trades and resident Den Mother, Molly, used to want to tear her hair out when we submitted drink menu changes with titles that chewed up enough printed real estate to require font size changes. The name for this rendition of an Old Fashioned, aromatic and herb-forward, is, of course, the catchphrase uttered by Tyrion Lannister, the character played by Peter Dinklage in *Game of Thrones*, and often appropriated by every first-year bartender who thinks themself a smooth operator.

INSTRUCTIONS ─────────────

1. Combine the bourbon, Bénédictine, allspice dram, and Bolivar bitters in a mixing glass. Stir gently until the ice begins to melt, 15 to 20 revolutions. Strain over a whiskey rock in a large rocks glass.

2. To garnish, briefly scorch the rosemary with a kitchen torch and top the drink with the herb.

   Note: To scale up for four people, use 6 ounces (168 ml) bourbon, 3 ounces (84 ml) Bénédictine, 2 ounces (56 ml) allspice dram, and ½ ounce (14 ml) Bolivar bitters.

   *There is no good substitute for these bitters; if you are unable to find them, simply omit this ingredient.

Smoked Sazerac

2 ounces (56 ml) Old Overholt Rye or other fine rye

¼ ounce (7 ml) Demerara Simple Syrup (page 181)

5 dashes bitters, such as Peychaud's Aromatic Bitters

Ice cubes

1 dash Smoked Absinthe Rinse (page 174)

MAKES 1 COCKTAIL

Like every parent that claims they don't have a favorite child, I could tell you that I love all of the cocktails in this chapter equally—but that's simply not true. There's something about Spencer's rendition of a Sazerac, the cocktail that defines New Orleans—one of the most inspiring, celebratory cities on planet Earth—that really tugs at my Northern Soul. Maybe it's something about the fact that New Orleans is at the end of the river that finds its source in my home state. Maybe it's because this is the drink I want to sip in a hammock, on a beach, or next to a campfire. The light element of smoke added to the absinthe certainly sets it apart from most other renditions, but the gentle, focused craft of creating one says something about the reason it has stood the test of time. From the simple act of rinsing the glass with a splash of the smoked absinthe to the counted dashes of Peychaud's Bitters to the blissful act of stirring the drink until the ice begins to gloss over and mellow the burn of the Overholt Rye, it's easy—after that first sip—to taste the storied history of American cocktail culture and celebrate it with gratitude.

INSTRUCTIONS ————————————

1. Combine the rye, simple syrup, and bitters in a mixing glass, then fill with ice. Stir until the ice begins to melt, 15 to 20 revolutions.

2. Rinse a serving glass with the absinthe rinse by rolling a very small amount around the inside of the glass, just enough to get the aroma. Strain the cocktail into the rinsed glass. This cocktail is traditionally served neat.

Note: To scale up for four people, use 8 ounces (235 ml) rye, 1 ounce (28 ml) simple syrup, and 1 ounce (28 ml) bitters.

THE REVERSE SAZERAC

While Absinthe is often an acquired taste, once that taste is acquired, you'll find yourself looking for more and more opportunities to savor it. A popular, heavy-duty rendition of the Sazerac involves reversing the proportions of whiskey and absinthe—essentially washing the glass with bourbon or rye and mixing the remaining ingredients with absinthe. I recommend trying one. Just one. They pack a wicked wallop.

Smoked Absinthe Rinse

2 cups (475 ml) absinthe

1 teaspoon (5 ml) liquid smoke

MAKES 2 CUPS (475 ML)

Absinthe was a liqueur wildly popular with the Bohemian crowd of nineteenth-century Europe. Poets, painters, musicians, performers, and bon vivants of all stripes kept it close at hand and made it part of their salacious and celebratory ventures. It's no wonder that it became a staple of New Orleans sipping parlors. The idea of incorporating the aroma of woodsmoke into absinthe was born as much out of its storied history, imagining raucous music, peals of laughter, fine tobacco, and roaring fireplaces, as it was because that flavor permeates a lot of what we do at my restaurants. Liquid smoke is readily found online or at big-box stores, where you can get a few ounces in a glass bottle for less than two bucks. Go easy. The flavor is powerful. Instead of invoking the genteel aroma of a drawing room of times gone by, you'll feel like you're sucking licorice schnapps in the cinders of a burned-down cabin.

INSTRUCTIONS ──────────

1. Combine the absinthe and liquid smoke and stir. Store in a glass jar in a cool, dry place.

HOW TO FALL IN LOVE
WITH A BASIC BATCH

Batching cocktails isn't cheating, nor is it really a life-hack. It's a calculated, common sense play when hosting even a modest gathering of folks interested in celebrating liquid finery. Any alcoholic drink poured with more than two ingredients is an opportunity to make your event an easy engagement and allow you to spend more time with your good company. In addition, everyone will get the same drink every time, regardless of diminished skills and good judgment in assessing proportions. The batch recipes supplied in this chapter will allow for four classic portions of each cocktail. If you are entertaining more guests or plan on pouring several more rounds, it's just a matter of arithmetic. Not having to measure, shake, and stir every drink for guests who are consuming at different rates allows you more time to take part in conversations, to entertain, and to be entertained. As my friend JD Fratzke often says, "Hospitality is the art of helping people celebrate their lives. How can you do that well if you're not celebrating your own?"

#Dope

1¼ ounces (35 ml) Maker's Mark
46 bourbon

1 ounce (28 ml) amaretto,
such as Lazzaroni Amaretto

¾ ounce (21 ml) sweet vermouth,
such as Carpano Antica Formula

3 dashes bitters, such as Fee Brothers
Whiskey Barrel–Aged Bitters

Ice cubes

1 thin orange slice, to garnish

Sugar, to garnish

MAKES 1 COCKTAIL

A few years back, we had a regular who would perch himself at the bar whenever Spencer was working—and only when Spencer was working. He'd ask for an updated improvisation on a standard East Coast supper club cocktail known as The Godfather, essentially a Manhattan flavored with a splash of amaretto. Each night this regular came in, he challenged Spencer to improve the previous evening's attempt: more this, less that, "what if we try a little (insert random cordial here) . . ." You get the picture. The regular was particularly impressed one night when Spencer held a lighter up to the orange peel he squeezed over the glass and the aromatic oils ignited in a quick flash. Thereafter, some form of fire became a requisite for the preparation of the cocktail, which eventually led to Spencer's idea of gently torching a layer of sugar sprinkled over a thinly sliced orange coin to create a brulée effect. Throughout all of these efforts, whenever said night's concoction was set down in front of this regular, he would take the first sip, savor it, and, without fail, remark, "That's dope." This rendition of the cocktail stuck around, though, sadly, the regular who inspired it did not. As an homage to his memory and the time we were able to spend with him, there was never really any question as to what we would name the drink he helped us make.

INSTRUCTIONS —————————

1. Combine the bourbon, amaretto, sweet vermouth, and bitters in a mixing glass, then fill with ice. Stir until the ice begins to melt, about 15 to 20 revolutions. Strain over a whiskey rock in a large rocks glass.

2. Make a brûlée orange coin garnish by laying the orange slice flat on an inflammable surface. Sprinkle a layer of sugar on top of the orange. Use a kitchen torch to heat the sugar until it begins to bubble and caramelize. Allow time for the sugar to cool, then place the coin flat on top of the whiskey rock and serve.

Note: To scale up for four people, use 5 ounces (168 ml) bourbon, 4 ounces (112 ml) amaretto, 3 ounces (84 ml) sweet vermouth, and 12 dashes bitters.

Coffee-Infused Boulevardier

1½ ounces (42 ml) Four Roses Bourbon or other fine bourbon

¾ ounce (21 ml) Coffee-Infused Campari (see below)

½ ounce (14 ml) sweet vermouth, such as Carpano Antica Formula

2 dashes orange bitters, such as Regans' Orange Bitters

1 large ice cube

Orange peel, to garnish

3 coffee beans, to garnish

MAKES 1 COCKTAIL

Spencer loves this one, particularly because of the coffee-infused Campari that is such a huge part of its personality. And given that much of Spencer's personality is coffee-infused, we love him, too. We highly recommend that you introduce coffee-infused Campari to your home liquor collection—just like Regans' Orange Bitters. Based on a recipe found in Charles H. Baker's *The Gentleman's Companion*, a globe-trotter's compendium of food and drink published in 1947, the orange bitters can be found in specialty stores or online. During warmer months, substitute your favorite gin for the Four Roses Bourbon and you'll have yourself a phenomenal Negroni custom made for skipping the nap usually involved with day-drinking.

INSTRUCTIONS ————————

1. Combine the bourbon, Campari, sweet vermouth, and orange bitters in a mixing glass, then fill with ice. Stir until the ice begins to melt, 15 to 20 revolutions. Strain over a whiskey rock in a large rocks glass. Serve garnished with an orange peel and the coffee beans.

   Note: To scale up for four people, use 6 ounces (168 ml) bourbon, 3 ounces (84 ml) Coffee-Infused Campari, 2 ounces (56 ml) sweet vermouth, and 8 dashes orange bitters.

1 cup (80 g) coffee beans

17 ounces (1½ L) Campari

MAKES ABOUT 2 CUPS (500 ML)

COFFEE-INFUSED CAMPARI

During the warmer months of the year, this infusion makes for an excellent brunch Negroni, although it's also lovely on the rocks by itself, with a splash of soda, or with a light pour of tequila. This stuff is magic and encourages the North Country art of the "double header," which is what we call day-drinking, eating dinner, then drinking again—all without a nap in between.

INSTRUCTIONS ————————

1. Combine the coffee and Campari. Let steep in a cool, dry place for 24 hours; do not oversteep. Strain through a fine-mesh strainer or a cheesecloth. Store in a glass jar in a cool, dry place.

The Bourbon Slushy

2 quarts (1.9 L) water

4 black tea bags

1 quart (1 L) fresh orange juice

1 quart (1 L) fresh lemon juice

¾ cup (75 g) sugar

2 cups (475 ml) bourbon

½ ounce (14 ml) bitters, such as Fee Brother's Whiskey Barrel–Aged Bitters

16 ounces (475 ml) ginger beer

MAKES ABOUT 25 SLUSHIES— ENOUGH FOR A PARTY

The original general manager at Handsome Hog introduced us to this cocktail shortly after we opened to the public. This was a cocktail his grandmother would make with brandy whenever the family gathered for Christmas. It took about two heartbeats for me to ask if we could try it with bourbon instead, because, well . . . bourbon. Grandma's Christmas cocktail became our most popular warm-weather favorite, and when Handsome Hog moved to its current location and built a patio with outdoor seating, we needed to start buying miniature mason jars in bulk.

INSTRUCTIONS

1. Combine the water and tea, bring it to a boil, and let steep for about 10 minutes. Add the orange juice, lemon juice, sugar, and bitters and stir to combine well.

2. Pour the mixture into pint mason jars, leaving room for a splash of ginger beer later. Freeze until solid. When you are about ready to serve, remove from the freezer and pour a splash of ginger beer over the top of each jar. Serve in the mason jars with a spoon.

Demerara Simple Syrup

2 cups (200 g) demerara sugar

2 cups (475 ml) water

MAKES 2 CUPS (475 ML)

Demerara sugar is made from raw cane sugar and can usually be found in the baking aisle of most supermarkets and co-ops. Don't just stuff those little packages from the coffee shop in your pockets without asking.

INSTRUCTIONS ————————

1. Combine equal parts demerara sugar and water in a saucepan. Bring to a boil, stirring until the sugar dissolves. Let cool, then store in a glass jar in the refrigerator for up to 3 weeks.

Tobacco-Infused Bénédictine

2 cups (475 ml) Bénédictine D.O.M.

1 generous teaspoon (2 g)
loose tobacco

MAKES 2 CUPS (475 ML)

The key to this recipe is the timing of the infusion. Do not let the tobacco soak in the Bénédictine too long or the drink will become unpleasantly bitter. Rather than sipping on a cocktail that reminds a cigar-lover of the comforting aroma of a walk-in humidor, an over-infusion will taste more like licking a dirty ashtray.

INSTRUCTIONS ————————

1. Combine the Bénédictine and tobacco in a glass jar and let it steep in a cool, dry place for 24 hours; do not oversteep. Strain through a fine-mesh strainer or a cheesecloth. Store in a glass jar in a cool, dry place.

DESSERTS

9

When it comes to entertaining, planning and preparation make for easy execution and maximum enjoyment. The more you're able to check off your list ahead of the first guests arriving, the more time you have to enjoy their company—and you theirs. A good deal of my time entertaining is spent with a glass or bottle of high-test inebriate in the palm of my hand. Since you and I are probably very much alike in that way, we both know the perils of trying to execute anything well (particularly good judgment) by the time the evening is winding down, and the digestion of the main course is finally allowing everyone present to consider the consumption of something sweet to punctuate the meal. In my experience, I've found that the best way to navigate that situation is to have desserts at the ready, set them out to self-serve, and let the chips fall where they may.

I admit, however, that I'm not a huge dessert guy. I never really had the patience for pastry production and, quite frankly, I'd rather crush a donut while hungover than savor crème caramel with a tiny spoon at the end of a tasting menu. I realize that I am out of the ordinary in that aspect. Since I firmly believe that entertaining is about meeting and exceeding the expectations of one's guests and fellow celebrators, I serve desserts when I throw a party. You should, too.

Super Easy Peanut Butter Banana Pudding

5-ounce (141 g) pack instant vanilla pudding

2 cups (475 ml) whole milk

8 ounces (225 g) cream cheese, at room temperature

⅔ cup (173 g) creamy peanut butter

8 ounces (226 g) Cool Whip or other store-bought whipped topping

1 cup (235 ml) heavy cream

2 tablespoons (15 g) powdered sugar

1 teaspoon pure vanilla extract

1 cup (80 g) crumbled store-bought vanilla wafers

3 bananas, thinly sliced

MAKES 6 INDIVIDUAL PUDDINGS

These puddings, served individually in glasses or jars, are a champion choice for the kind of gathering you know is going to last into the wee hours. They are so easy to make and store, chilled, ahead of time, and to simply unwrap and set out on the table with a pile of spoons and paper napkins. Tap into your next-level hosting skills by finding out if there are any nut allergies on your guest list. If so, this dessert can be made safely and deliciously without the peanut butter, so long as you're sure to use clean utensils for the different preparations. A classy way to differentiate between the peanut butter and nut-free renditions is to serve each in a different style glass. For instance: peanut butter version in a lowball and the nut-free version in a martini glass.

INSTRUCTIONS ───────────

1. Combine the pudding mix and milk in a mixing bowl and whisk until smooth. With an electric mixer in a separate bowl, beat the cream cheese with the peanut butter until smooth, then fold in the Cool Whip. In a third bowl, beat the heavy cream, powdered sugar, and vanilla until the cream forms soft peaks.

2. Set six rocks glasses, lowball glasses, or mason jars on a countertop. Use one-third of the vanilla wafers to line the bottoms of the glasses or jars. Top with half of the peanut butter and cream cheese mixture, then half of the banana slices, followed by half of the vanilla pudding. Repeat the layers one more time, then top with whipped topping, the remaining banana slices. Sprinkle the remaining vanilla wafers over the tops. Store in your refrigerator until ready to serve.

Stewed Peaches and Bourbon Over Cornbread

STEWED PEACHES

6 ripe peaches, peeled, pitted, and cut into wedges

¼ cup (50 g) white sugar

¼ cup (56 g) packed light brown sugar

¼ cup (60 ml) water

1 tablespoon (15 ml) fresh lemon juice

1½ teaspoons pure vanilla extract

1 teaspoon ground cinnamon

BOURBON WHIPPED CREAM

1 cup (235 ml) heavy cream

3 tablespoons (45 ml) bourbon

2 tablespoons (15 g) powdered sugar

½ teaspoon freshly grated nutmeg

6 Cornbread Muffins (page 84)

SERVES 6

This recipe is a great way to celebrate two forms of deliciousness I love the most: ripe peaches and bourbon whiskey. It's also a superb use of cornbread muffins left over from last night's party—assuming there are any. It's okay if you have to bake some specifically for this dessert.

INSTRUCTIONS

1. To make the peaches, combine the peaches, white and brown sugars, water, lemon juice, vanilla, and cinnamon in a medium saucepan. Bring to a boil over medium-high heat, stirring to dissolve the sugars, then reduce the heat to a simmer. Cook for about 5 minutes, until the peaches are tender but still hold their shapes. Remove from the heat and allow to cool slightly.

2. To make the whipped cream, combine the cream, bourbon, powdered sugar, and nutmeg in a mixing bowl and whip with an electric mixer until the cream forms soft peaks.

3. To serve, split the muffins in half and divide among 6 dessert bowls. Spoon the peach mixture over the muffins. Top with a dollop of the bourbon whipped cream. Garnish, if you'd like, with toasted nuts, crispy bacon pieces, caramel popcorn, fresh berries, or whatever the hell you want.

Kinda Healthy Bourbon Pecan Pie
with Maple Whip

PIE CRUST

2½ cups (313 g) all-purpose
flour, plus more for dusting

2 teaspoons sugar

2 teaspoons kosher salt

¾ cup (165 g) cold unsalted butter,
cut into pea-sized pieces

½ cup (103 g) cold lard,
cut into pea-sized pieces, preferably,
or vegetable shortening

½ cup (120 ml) ice-cold water

FILLING

1 cup (225 g) packed dark brown sugar

½ cup (160 g) pure maple syrup

3 eggs

¼ cup (60 ml) melted unsalted butter

¼ cup (60 ml) bourbon

2 teaspoons pure vanilla extract

½ teaspoon kosher salt

2 cups (224 g) toasted pecan halves

TOPPING

1 cup (235 ml) heavy cream

¼ cup (80 g) pure maple syrup

**MAKES 1
(9-INCH [23 CM]) PIE**

This dessert represents what my journey in food has been all about: paying respect and homage to the Southern food I love while infusing it with flavors and ingredients from my home in the North. While pecan pie may be one of the most storied pastries in American cuisine south of the Ohio River, maple syrup is a North Country birthright—a springtime gift from Mother Nature savored by those who have chosen to live in the North for hundreds, if not thousands, of years.

INSTRUCTIONS ———————

1. To make the pie crust, combine the flour, sugar, salt, butter, and lard in a food processer and pulse in short, quick bursts, 8 to 10 times, until combined. Add the ice water and pulse 8 to 10 more times, until the dough sticks together when squeezed. Dump the crumbly dough into a bowl and refrigerate, covered with plastic wrap, for at least 30 minutes.

2. On a floured surface, roll out the dough into a 12-inch (30 cm)-round disc. Every few rolls, flip the dough over and dust flour so the pastry doesn't stick to the work surface. Transfer the rolled-out pastry to a 9-inch (23 cm) pie pan and trim the excess dough, leaving a 1-inch (2.5 cm) overhang. Crimp the edge of the dough, then chill the pie shell until firm, at least 15 minutes.

3. Preheat the oven to 350°F (177°C).

4. To make the filling, combine the brown sugar, maple syrup, eggs, butter, bourbon, vanilla, and salt, stirring to fully incorporate the eggs and sugar. Arrange the pecans on the pie shell.

5. Pour the mixture over the pecans and bake for 40 to 50 minutes, until the filling is dark brown and bubbly and the crust is golden brown around the edges.

6. Remove the pie from the oven and allow to cool at least 1 hour before serving.

7. Shortly before serving the pie, make the topping. Combine the heavy cream and maple syrup and whip with an electric mixer until the cream forms soft peaks. Slice the pie and top each slice with the whipped cream.

Beignets

1¼ teaspoons active dry yeast

⅓ cup (67 g) white sugar

¾ cup (175 ml) warm water

½ cup (120 ml) whole milk

1 egg, beaten

¾ teaspoon kosher salt

3½ cups (438 g) all-purpose flour

2 tablespoons (25 g) lard or
vegetable shortening

Oil for deep-frying

Powdered sugar, for dusting

Hickory Chocolate Sauce
(recipe opposite)

MAKES 16 TO 20
BEIGNETS

A lot of people are intimidated by the idea of taking on these classic Crescent City confections. Believe me, I understand! Between the delicate timing, the large amount of counter space needed for rolling out the dough, the hot oil you have to work with, and the powdered sugar that goes absolutely everywhere, it can seem like a lot to take on—especially if you're entertaining. That is why, like any of life's more important challenges, you need to make a plan and tackle it head on with your friends. Read the recipe through a few times and assemble all the ingredients, then make the dough and allow it to rise for the full 2 hours while you and your guests savor dinner. When the dishes are cleared, assemble your team, heat up the oil, assign each member a task (like brewing the chicory coffee or heating the cream), and roll out and cut the dough. Everyone will learn something, everyone will contribute, and everyone will share in the curse of powdered sugar on their dope party threads.

INSTRUCTIONS ───────────

1. Dissolve the yeast and white sugar in the warm water in a large mixing bowl. Let sit for 10 minutes.

2. Whisk in the milk, egg, and salt. Mix in half of the flour. Cut in the shortening. Add the remaining flour and mix with a spoon until the dough is not too sticky and can be shaped with your hands.

3. Turn the dough out onto a floured work surface and knead just until smooth. Place the dough in an oiled bowl, cover with a towel, and allow to rise in a warm spot of your kitchen for 2 hours. The dough will double in size.

4. On a heavily floured surface, roll out the dough until it is ¼-inch (6 mm) thick. Use a pizza slicer or knife to cut the dough into 2½-inch (6.4 cm) square pieces. Meanwhile, preheat the oil for deep-frying in a countertop deep-fryer or Dutch oven to 370°F (188°C). Set out a wire rack or line a sheet pan with paper towels.

5. Fry 3 to 4 pieces at a time in the oil. After carefully lowering the dough into the oil, wait a few moments until the dough floats to the surface, then flip each piece immediately. Allow to fry until the bottom is golden brown and puffy, about 3 minutes, before flipping again and continuing to cook until the other side is brown, about 2 minutes more. When golden brown on both sides, carefully remove from the oil using a slotted spoon or spider strainer and drain on the prepared wire rack or paper towels. Let cool until they are cool enough to handle.

6. Generously dust with powdered sugar, drizzle the sauce over, and serve.

¾ cup (175 ml) heavy cream

½ cup (100 g) sugar

6 ounces (175 g) dark chocolate, chopped

⅛ teaspoon kosher salt

¼ cup (60 ml) strongly brewed chicory coffee

½ teaspoon pure vanilla extract

MAKES 1 CUP (235 ML) OR ENOUGH FOR UP TO 24 BEIGNETS

CHICORY CHOCOLATE SAUCE

INSTRUCTIONS ───────

1. In a medium saucepan, heat the heavy cream over medium heat until simmering. Whisk in the sugar. Continue whisking until the sugar dissolves.

2. Take the cream off the heat and whisk in the chocolate until melted. Whisk in the salt, coffee, and vanilla. Serve warm over the beignets.

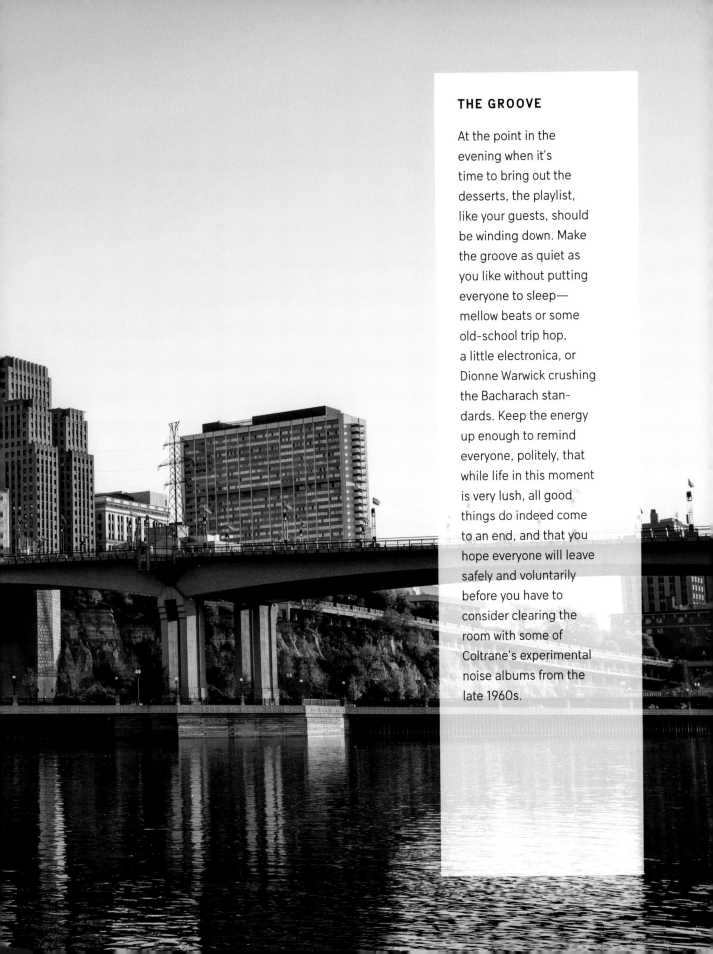

THE GROOVE

At the point in the evening when it's time to bring out the desserts, the playlist, like your guests, should be winding down. Make the groove as quiet as you like without putting everyone to sleep—mellow beats or some old-school trip hop, a little electronica, or Dionne Warwick crushing the Bacharach standards. Keep the energy up enough to remind everyone, politely, that while life in this moment is very lush, all good things do indeed come to an end, and that you hope everyone will leave safely and voluntarily before you have to consider clearing the room with some of Coltrane's experimental noise albums from the late 1960s.

ABOUT THE AUTHOR

Justin Sutherland is a nationally recognized cooking celebrity, chef, and entrepreneur who is the co-host of the nationally-syndicated *Fast Foodies*, a producer and host of *Taste the Culture*, an *Iron Chef* winner, and a contestant on *Top Chef* (season 16) and Guy Fieri's "Tournament of Champions." Justin is a successful entrepreneur who runs multiple restaurants in the Twin Cities, including the acclaimed pig-centric Southern restaurant, Handsome Hog; is the culinary consultant for Allianz Field, home of the MLS's Minnesota United FC; and also has a line of spices sold locally in grocery chains in the Upper Midwest, as well as signature whiskey blend with Tattersall Distilling. He is active in the social justice community and is the co-owner of Hybrid Nation, a socially conscious streetwear and lifestyle brand that promotes the importance of diversity and social equality, and is active in many Twin Cities philanthropic efforts, raising funds and donations for hospitality workers affected by the pandemic through The North Stands, MN Central Kitchen, and also as a board member the Inner City Ducks.

SPECIAL THANKS TO:

JD Fratzke

Matt Green

Patrick O'Hare

Spencer Pinche Short

INDEX

RESOURCES

Craftmade Aprons
craftmadeaprons.com
High-quality, stylish aprons and other kitchen apparel
for professionals and home cooks

Cry Baby Craig's Hot Sauce
crybabycraigs.com
Habanero-garlic hot sauce; the site has a list of retail locations,
or you can order direct from the site

Hybrid Nation
hybridnationclothing.com
Socially conscious clothing, accessories, and home goods
that promote diversity and justice

Justin Sutherland
justinsutherland.com
Signature spices, rubs, and whiskeys, and the latest news about Justin

ABOUT THE PHOTOGRAPHER

Minnesota native **Asha Belk** is a professional photographer who specializes in food and lifestyle photography. She is also a school social worker and incorporates the use of photography to enrich the lives of her students through imagery and art as self-expression. During her matriculation at Clark Atlanta University and New York University, she developed a passion for capturing authentic moments by sharing stories through her lens. Her work has been featured in *The Immigrant Cookbook*, *ELLE* magazine, *Billboard*, and on air with the Food Network and NBC Washington's "Inequality of America: A Call to Action." In 2021, her photography centered around the civil unrest following the death of George Floyd in Minneapolis that launched the first official exhibit at The Capri Theater's Carlson Family Foundation Art Gallery.

The Rondo Commemorative Plaza

We extend a sincere welcome to all who come to the Rondo Commemorative Plaza. Situated next to Interstate 94, this landmark has been created to honor the legacy of Rondo's African-American community which was destroyed by the freeway's construction. This is a space to remember, celebrate, and build goodwill among all who call the Rondo Neighborhood home.

Rondo Avenue, Inc., Board of Directors